IMAGES
of America

LIVERMORE

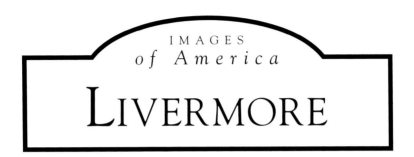

IMAGES
of America

LIVERMORE

Livermore Heritage Guild and John Christian

ARCADIA
PUBLISHING

Published by Arcadia Publishing
Charleston, South Carolina

Printed in the United States of America

Library of Congress Control Number: 2012943201

For all general information, please contact Arcadia Publishing:
Telephone 843-853-2070
Fax 843-853-0044
E-mail sales@arcadiapublishing.com
For customer service and orders:
Toll-Free 1-888-313-2665

Visit us on the Internet at www.arcadiapublishing.com

CONTENTS

ACKNOWLEDGMENTS

Bringing this book to publication, the Livermore Heritage Guild (LHG) collaborated with volunteer John Christian of the graduate school of Cal State East Bay. His enthusiasm for the subject, relentless drive, and organizational skills are the foundation of this work. LHG museum curator Don Smith connected us with John and was a tenacious editor. I would also like to acknowledge and publicly thank our research and editorial team: Gary Drummond, Alicia Eltgroth, Anne Homan, Susan and Bill Junk, Jeff Kaskey, Dick and Jean Lerche, Bria Reiniger, and Anna Siig. Laura Bowley, Chuck Eyler, and Nancy Wong contributed their talents to the enhancement of some of the photographs in this book. A big thanks goes to our editors at Arcadia, Jared Nelson and Tim Sumerel, for their encouragement, guidance, and patience through this process. The photographs and source materials can be found at the LHG History Center located at 2155 Third Street in the old Carnegie Library building. If you see yourself or someone you know in the images contained in this book, the LHG would love to hear about it. Visit us, call us (925.449.9927), or drop us a line (lhg@lhg.org or P.O. Box 961, Livermore, California, 94551). Check out our website at www.livermorehistory.com. We are always interested in more images from this time period, so please collaborate with us to "Save Yesterday for Tomorrow"—respectfully submitted by Loretta Kaskey, LHG project lead.

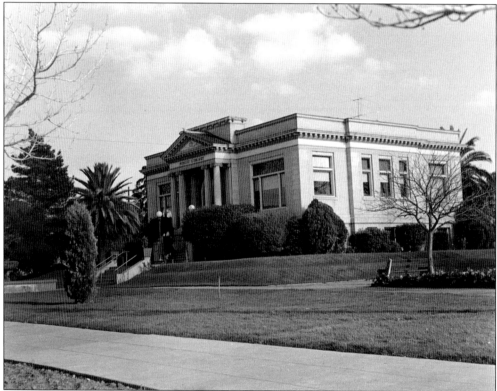

Livermore's Carnegie library at 2155 Third Street, built in a Classical Revival style and called a "temple in the park," was placed in the National Register of Historic Places in 2011, commemorating its centennial.

INTRODUCTION

Mid-century growth brought tremendous change to the Livermore Valley. In 1930, the population of Livermore was roughly 3,000. This population increased to 4,300 in 1950, and by 1965, there were 25,300 residents, due to the arrival of Lawrence Radiation Laboratory and Sandia Corporation in the early 1950s. The city responded with housing developments, schools, and the expansion of roads, sewer, police, and fire services.

Construction of the Tesla Portal section of the Hetch Hetchy project, from 1927 to its completion in December 1934, helped support the Livermore economy during the Depression. The 28.5-mile tunnel project through the Coast Range Mountains required concrete, steel, hauling, and local labor to achieve its goals. The construction headquarters for this effort was established at Railroad and L Streets.

Repeal of prohibition in 1933 brought viticulture back, along with the revitalization of local taverns, restaurants and associated businesses. The National Recovery Act (NRA), Civilian Work Administration (CWA), and Works Progress Administration (WPA) were projects of the 1930s that developed Livermore's infrastructure and downtown, attracted residents, and boosted employment. WPA construction expenditures were $264,649 between 1935 and 1937 alone. By the beginning of World War II, Livermore had renovated everything from sidewalks to city hall.

Livermore's first airport was established in 1929 by the Civil Aeronautics Administration to provide an alternate landing site to fog-prone San Francisco and Oakland. This airport was located just west of Rincon and south of Portola. During World War II, the navy operated the airport as well as the pilot-training facility of Livermore Naval Air Station. By war's end in 1947, the airport became known as Livermore Sky Ranch, and the Naval Air Station was converted to the University of California Radiation Laboratory.

The existing healthcare industries, including Livermore Sanitarium (mental health), Arroyo Del Valle Sanatorium (tuberculosis), the Livermore Division Veterans Administration Medical Center, and numerous private hospitals, were promoted as health shrines in the 1930s. A popular promotional campaign by the chamber of commerce claimed one could "Live Longer in Livermore." The 1950s saw the start of the Livermore 20-30 Club, which raised funds for a new hospital. Valley Memorial Hospital opened in 1961 on a site donated by Henry J. Kaiser where the Kaiser Paving Company once stood.

The Livermore Rodeo has become an institution since it began in 1918. The old rodeo grandstands at South Livermore and Pacific Avenues expanded to seat 10,000 in 1929. The slogan of "World's Fastest Rodeo" was first used in 1935 because of the fast action of events and the speed at which the next participant moved out of the chute. The grandstands at the old rodeo site were condemned and demolished in 1959. The current rodeo grounds in Robertson Park (named for Dr. John Robertson, founder of the Livermore Sanitarium) were built in 1967 and host more than 6,000 spectators annually.

This second Livermore book in the Images of America series highlights Livermore's mid-century growth. Celebrating families and individuals, industry and government, the downtown parade and the pageantry of the rodeo, the Livermore Heritage Guild shares these images from their extensive collection. Within each chapter, readers will find a small town and a modern city that evolved into today's Livermore.

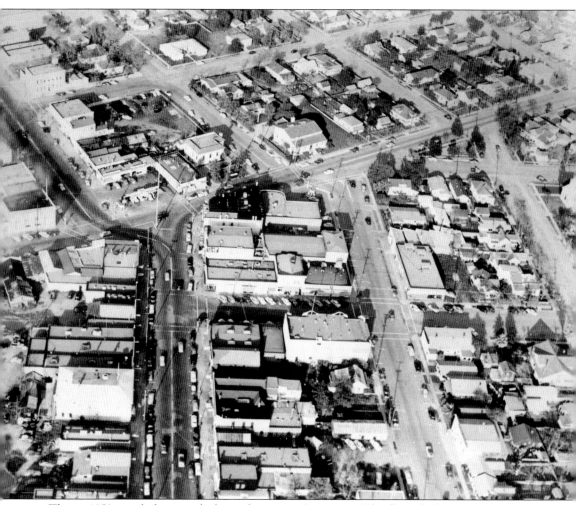

This c. 1950 aerial photograph shows downtown Livermore. The flagpole (center left) is in the middle of the First Street and Livermore Avenue intersection.

One

DOWNTOWN AND
AROUND TOWN

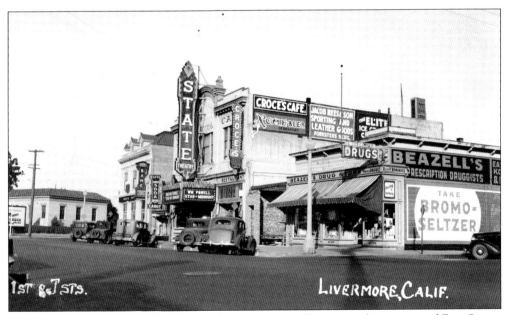

Downtown, with a 126-foot flagpole in the intersection of its namesake avenue and First Street, is the heart of the community. This mid-1930s postcard depicts the south side of First Street from J Street toward Livermore Avenue, facing east. The 1929 Pacific Telephone and Telegraph Company's repeater station (far left) cost $185,000. Toward the west (from left to right) are the Masonic Building (1909), New Deal Coffee Shoppe (1932), and Schenone Building (1914) with the entrance to the State Theater. These buildings still stand today.

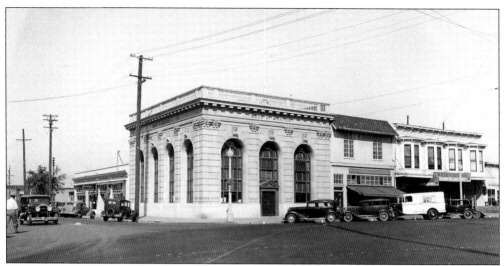

The Bank of Italy Building at 2250 First Street (above) and the Masonic Building (below) at 119 South Livermore Avenue diagonally anchor the intersection of Livermore Avenue and First Street. The Bank of Italy Building was constructed in 1922 and became Bank of America in 1930. The bank occupied the northeast corner until 1957. An excellent example of the Beaux-Arts style, it is in the National Register of Historic Places (1978). On the far left in the c. 1935 Lawless Drug postcard above is the C.H. Rasmussen 1913 post office building. The Masonic Building at the southwest corner, shown below about 1950, was designed by local architect Julius L. Weilbye and erected in 1909. Tenants have included a bank and saloon/billiard hall. The Masons still own and use the building.

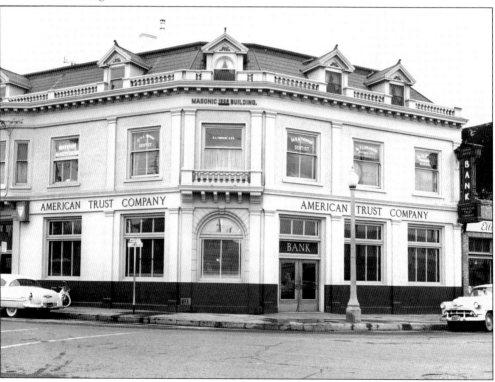

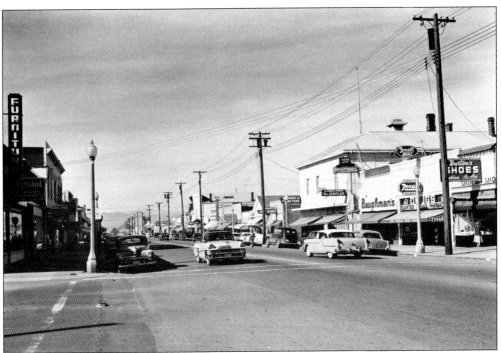

Looking west along the north side of First Street (above) from the intersection at J Street, the buildings in this c. 1955 photograph are still visible today. From left to right are the 1915 Building, Odd Fellows Building (enlarged in 1874), and the Carlisle 2 Building (1932). In the 1950s, Livermore began to develop at a rapid pace. The population grew between 1950 and 1960 from less than 5,000 to over 16,000. Below about 1955 is First Street from Livermore Avenue looking west along the south side of the street. The Schenone Building looms in the foreground on the left.

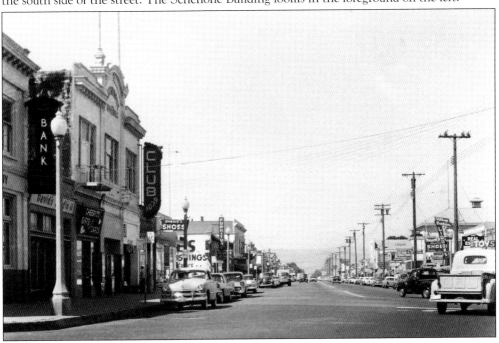

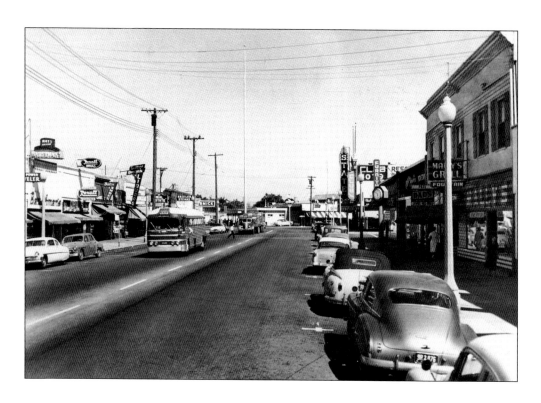

The c. 1954 photograph above, facing east along the south side, shows First Street near K Street. To the middle right, the State Theatre sign hangs out from the Schenone Building. It was built in 1914 by Louis Schenone, an Italian immigrant who married Robert Livermore Jr.'s daughter Katherine. Joseph Schenone, Louis's nephew, was an elected judge in Livermore, serving from 1952 to 1973. In the foreground, a bus hums along, probably headed to the Greyhound station on L Street. Below, an opposing view of First Street, about 1954, looks east from K Street toward the flagpole at the intersection of Livermore Avenue. The Hagstrom Building (built in 1932) is shown in the lower left side in this Lawless Drug postcard image as a "5-10-15 Cent Store." Backlit, neon, and nonuniform signage made a colorful and haphazard display on mid-century First Street.

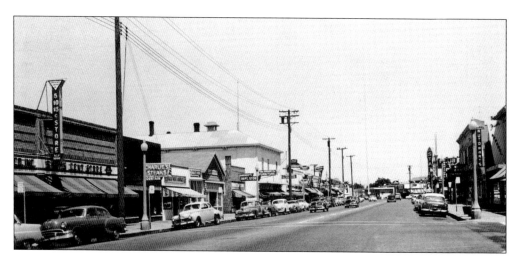

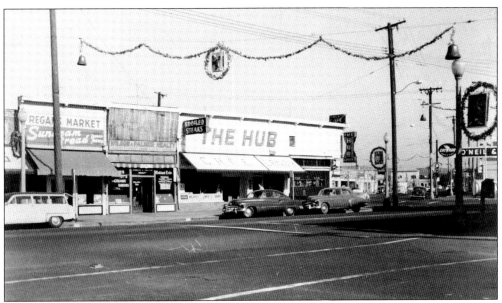

Pictured above about 1955, the Hub, located on the northwest corner of First Street and Livermore Avenue, was a popular saloon as early as the 1880s, but was off-limits to naval air station servicemen in the 1940s. In 1946, two former servicemen, Homer L. Leister and Lewis D. Woodle, opened the Hub Café, featuring steak and chicken dinners. Tex Spruiell opened a candy store in the Hub Café in 1955. Below, the Hub is pictured in the 1960s on Livermore Avenue, looking north. To the far left in the photograph is the Carlisle Building, erected in 1928. The taxi office seen on the Livermore Avenue side of the Hub was moved there in 1953. The Hub was torn down in the mid-1970s. Lizzie Fountain Park is now on the site.

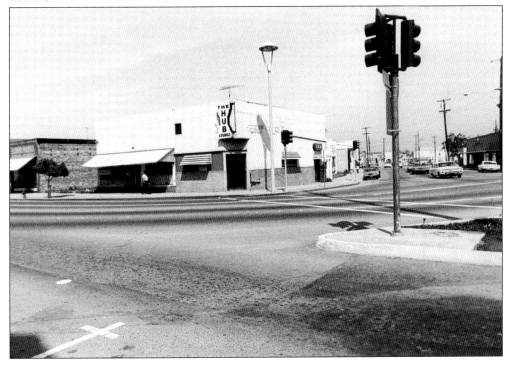

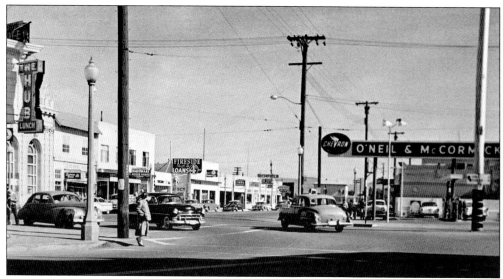

First Street at Livermore Avenue is visible in this view facing east about 1950. This photograph was taken from The Hub. The O'Neil & McCormick Chevron on the southeast corner replaced the Livermore Hotel in 1928, reflecting the city's growing auto traffic. Mills Square Park occupies the site today. Stripes around the bottom of the flagpole were intended to keep drivers from crashing into it.

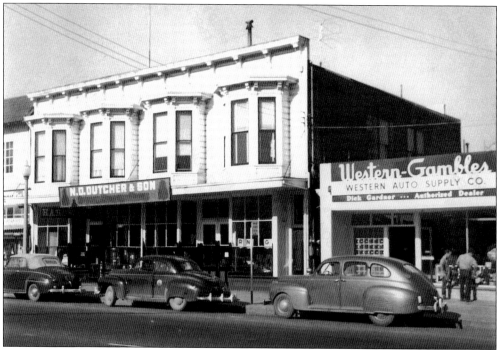

Dutcher's Hardware is pictured around 1950 on East First Street east of the Bank of Italy Building. Operated at the time by Norris Dutcher Jr., the store saw steady business. Dutcher's son "Dutch" Dutcher sold the business in 1959. With the exception of the Bank of Italy, all the buildings seen in the photographs on this page were torn down to provide for the current streetscape around the Bankhead Theater.

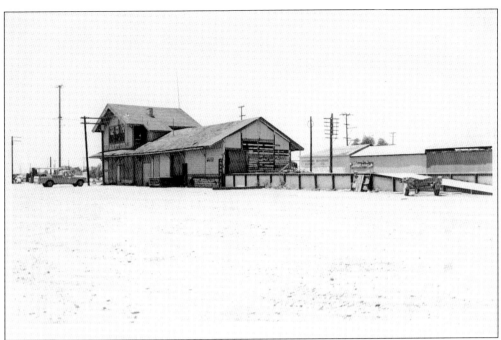

Since 1892, Livermore's Southern Pacific Depot was a center for freight and passenger traffic. Passenger service was discontinued in 1941, and the building was closed and condemned in 1973. The tracks would be realigned north of the existing location. A group of concerned citizens mobilized to save the landmark, and the Livermore Heritage Guild was born.

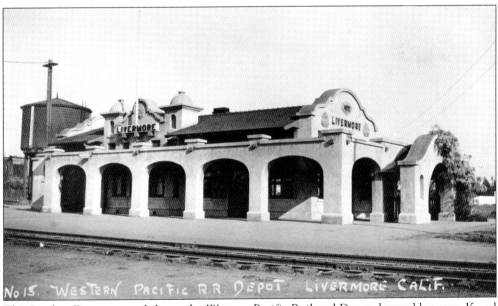

This Lawless Drug postcard shows the Western Pacific Railroad Depot, located between K and L Streets on Railroad Avenue. The depot was built in 1908 for $10,000 in the Mission Revival architectural style typical of other California Western Pacific depots. The depot provided passenger service until 1951 and was torn down in 1967.

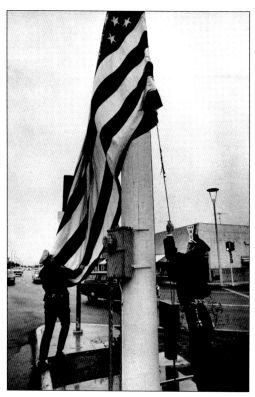

Livermore police officers raise the flag in the late 1960s. In 1905, Livermore citizens bought a 126-foot-tall flagpole and proudly raised it in the intersection of First Street and Livermore Avenue. As cars replaced horses, the flagpole became the bane of motorists. In 1959, it was moved 15 feet and out of the intersection. Despite being hit by cars 61 times between 1931 and 1972, the flagpole remained standing, finally retiring in 2004.

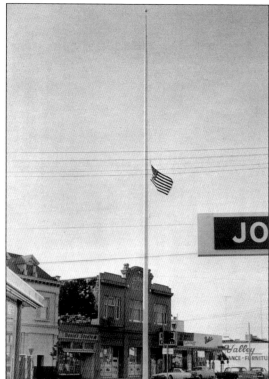

The historic Livermore flagpole shows the flag at half-mast following the assassination of Pres. John F. Kennedy in 1963.

Two

BUSINESS AND INDUSTRY

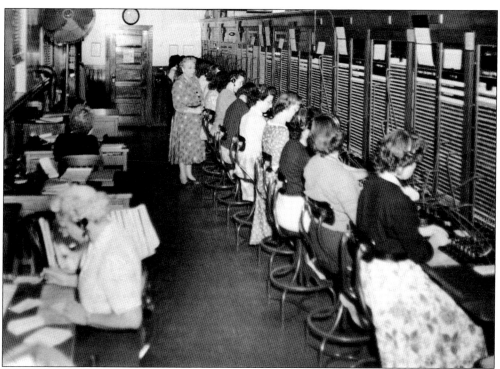

Telephone exchanges hired local single women to staff switchboards, visible in this c. 1950 photograph. In 1953, Pacific Telephone and Telegraph Company on South Livermore Avenue at Second Street (built in 1929 and closed in 1956) held an open house that attracted over 1,000 Livermore residents. Switchboard and civil defense phone line demonstrations were conducted. An average of 7,180 phone calls a day were placed through these switchboards.

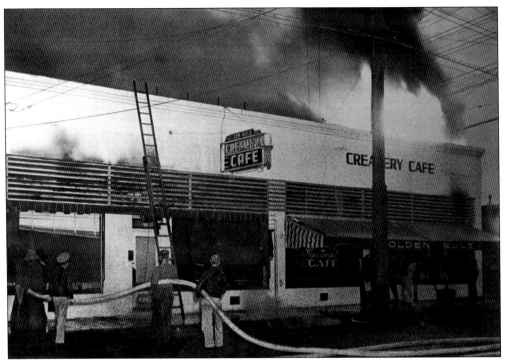

A 1949 fire at the Creamery, at the northeast corner of J and Second Streets, was not enough to put the popular restaurant out of business. Having lost her husband the same year, owner Vettie Mize continued to serve up some of the best "home-cooked" meals around. The restaurant is still remembered fondly by many residents who visited as teenagers. The business was sold in 1957.

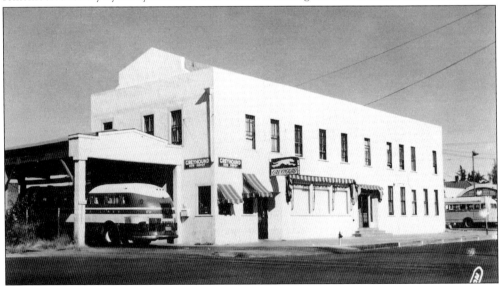

The Greyhound Bus Depot, pictured about 1960 on the east side of L Street between Railroad Avenue and First Street, served the Livermore valley from 1923 to 1962. Originally the Farmers Exchange (built 1873), the building was remodeled and converted into the Traveler's Hotel in 1923. It became the Lutz Hotel in the 1950s, as Arnold Lutz ran the Greyhound depot. The building was torn down in 1967.

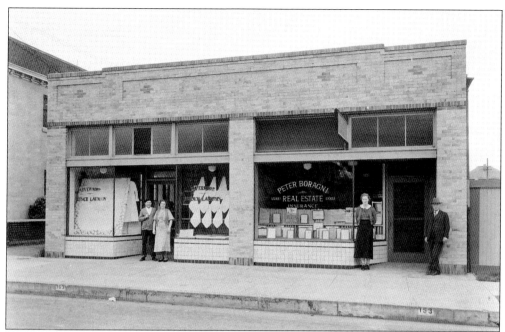

Mr. and Mrs. Gerald LaFon operate the Livermore French Laundry, and an unidentified woman stands with Peter Boragni of Peter Boragni Real Estate and Insurance in this c. 1930 photograph. This classic example of mid-century commercial vernacular architecture with recessed doorways flanked by deep display windows, transoms, and decorative brick was erected in 1930 on South L Street. Living near the Livermore Airport, Boragni offered a $5,000 policy "against falling airplanes" and "objects that fell out of planes."

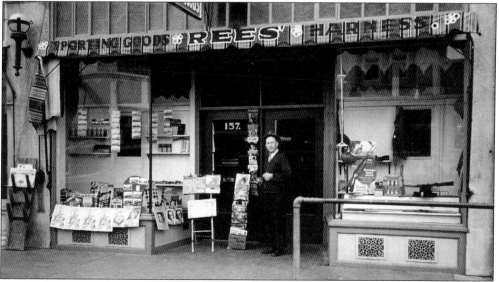

A man pauses for the camera about 1935 at the entrance to H.J. Rees' Sporting Goods on the street level of the Forester's Building (built 1914) at the northwest corner of J and Second Streets. Jacob Rees started a harness shop in 1889 and died in 1919. By the 1930s, the H.J. Rees & Sons store advertised sporting and hunting goods. The family business survived for 62 years, closing in 1951.

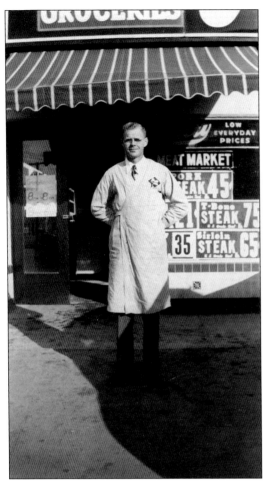

Hank Stratmann is pictured about 1950 outside the 1941 Purity store at First and L Streets. The *Livermore Herald* enthuses: "a reinforced concrete structure of the most modern design. The entire west side of the building is plate glass, providing full-store display and natural light which augments the battery of floodlights inside and outside the store." When Purity closed in 1959, architect Hans J. Schiller divided the space and gave it the Googie style it has today.

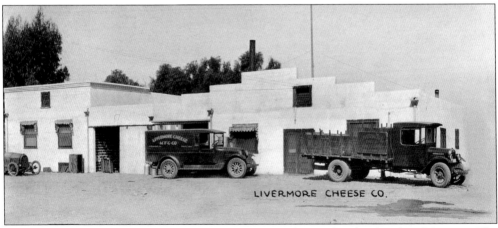

Livermore Cheese Company is pictured about 1925 on the north side of Railroad Avenue. The company was run by the Calderoni brothers Charles and Salvador, natives of Italy, who brought a method for making cheese with them to Livermore in the 1920s. The operation was expanded in 1936 with the opening of a second plant in Tracy. The Livermore Cheese Company manufactured Monterey cheese through the 1930s.

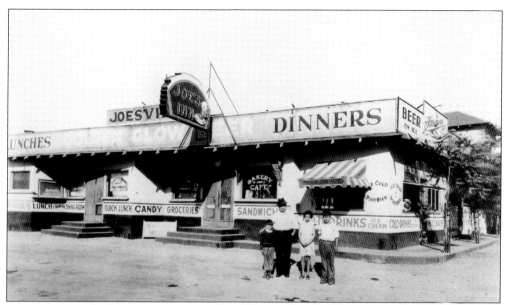

Joseville was built about 1925 on Portola Avenue near L Street. During Prohibition, "a little bootlegging" went on here. The Joseville Club attracted servicemen during the war and visitors every summer to see the country and western bands that played during rodeo season. From left to right (standing) are Richard Caratti and his father, Joe, sister, Anita, and brother, Albert. Albert later tended bar in the club.

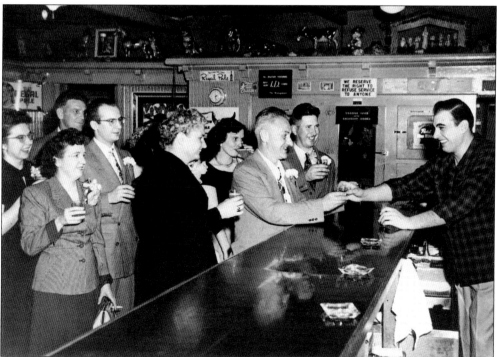

Joseville Club is pictured in 1952 with a party in progress. The bartender is Albert Carrati, Joe's son. Like his father, Albert was also a popular character in town. Of the porcelain figurines along the top of the cabinet, one set appears to be Snow White and the Seven Dwarfs.

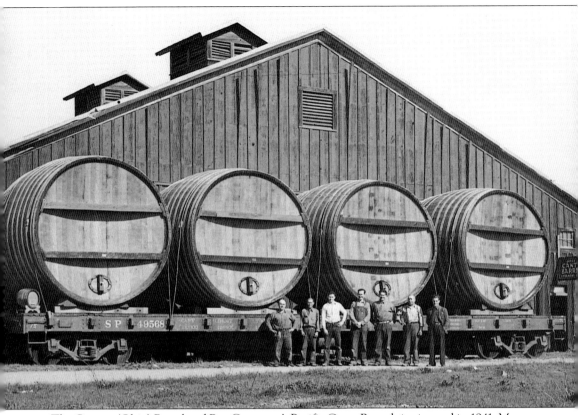

The Canton (Ohio) Barrel and Bag Company's Pacific Coast Branch is pictured in 1941. Manager Paul Martia stands far right next to foreman Ernest Ciglitui in front of four 6,300-gallon redwood barrels on the Southern Pacific rails. The factory was located on the north side of Railroad Avenue between North P and North N Streets and employed five other workers—from left to right, Leonard Panella, Mato Rebusa, Russell Devaney, Joseph Harworth, and William Tusa. Previously, this trackside warehouse contained the Pioneer Winery.

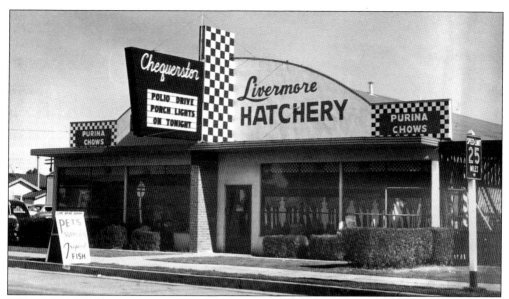

Ed Van Ormer and Burt Duke opened the Livermore Hatchery at the northeast corner of North L Street and Railroad Avenue in 1953. Van Ormer was associated with Castro Valley's poultry industry. Duke built a fryer production facility in Livermore, raising 48,000 chickens a year. The Livermore Hatchery began as a facility that incubated eggs then expanded into a feed and pet supply store. By 1956, it changed focus from poultry and pets to furniture. The Chequerstor sold "interior effects" for the new suburban homes. Below is the interior of Livermore's Hatchery about 1955. On field trips, children would delight in playing with baby chicks that were just days out of the incubators. Burt Duke (owner) is shown on the left.

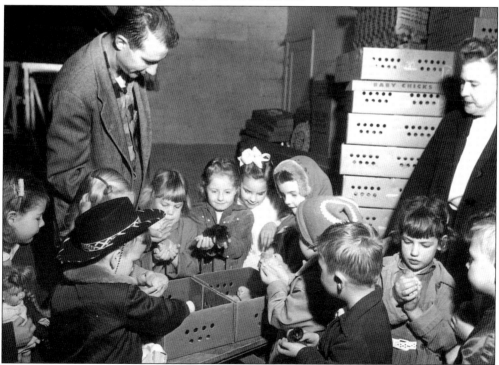

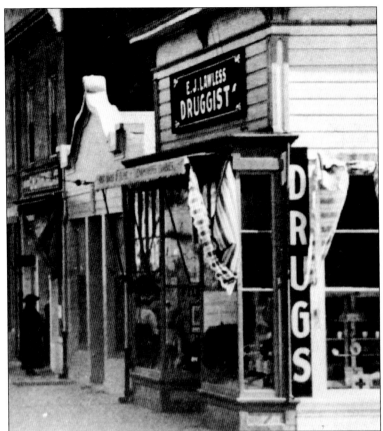

This early-1920s image shows Lawless Drugs at the southeast corner of First and K Streets. E.J. Lawless bought and renamed Beck's Drugs in 1917. He organized Livermore Boy Scout Troop No. 1 in 1921 and also dabbled in photography. His store printed and developed real-photo postcards from customer negatives, several of which are featured throughout this book. Lawless sold his store in 1941.

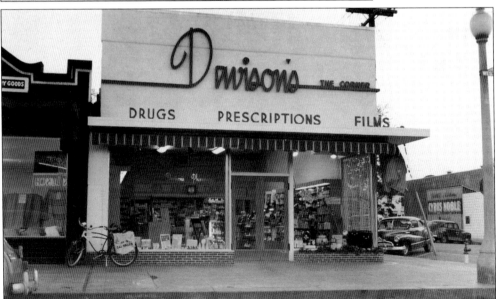

Davison's Pharmacy, pictured about 1950, was located at the southeast corner of First and K Streets. Formerly Lawless's drugstore, it became Davison's Pharmacy in 1941. Davison's moved in the 1960s to the East Avenue shopping center.

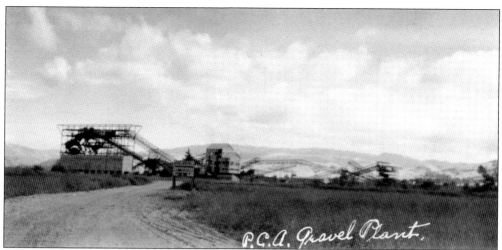

Sand and gravel are essential ingredients for construction—roads, freeways, dams, bridges, schools, buildings, hospitals, and homes—and Livermore Valley provided these resources to build the San Francisco Bay Area. Pacific Concrete and Aggregate (PCA) gravel plant, pictured above about 1940, began operation in the Livermore Valley in 1927. In 1946, PCA reported owning 1,425 acres west of Livermore, with reserve aggregates of 58 million tons. Kaiser Construction Company secured options for 26 acres of the Arthur Holm property in the Mocho Creek area in 1923. This site was abandoned in 1933 and donated to the city as the site for Valley Memorial Hospital. Kaiser expanded operations in 1931 one mile east of Pleasanton. That facility was called Radum after a train stop nearby. Radum occupied 600 acres and could produce 1,000 tons of aggregate every hour. Below is a c. 1955 Henry J. Kaiser Radum Plant promotional image.

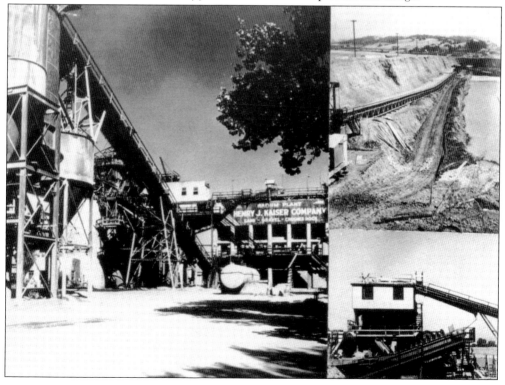

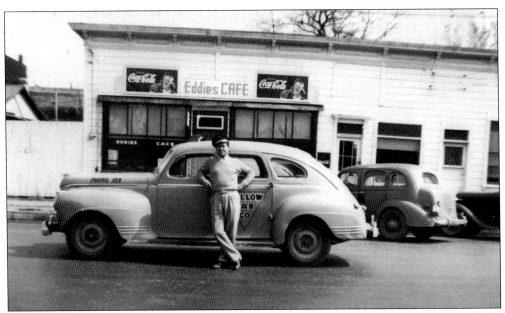

The *Livermore Herald* first mentions taxi service in 1919 (H.B. O'Donnell from San Francisco had a fleet of Fords). Above, a driver poses with his yellow cab in front of Eddies Café on South K Street about 1945. The café in the background was owned by H.A. and Willie Mae Eddington. During the 1940s, cabs like this one shuffled Navy personnel to and from town. The city designated four parking spaces for taxis on South K Street between First and Second Streets. Below, an unidentified woman poses with a Livermore Valley cab at the taxi stop on South K Street between First and Second Streets about 1945. The city had a taxicab ordinance in 1950 that set a maximum fare in town at 50¢, with a $4-per-hour charge for waiting time.

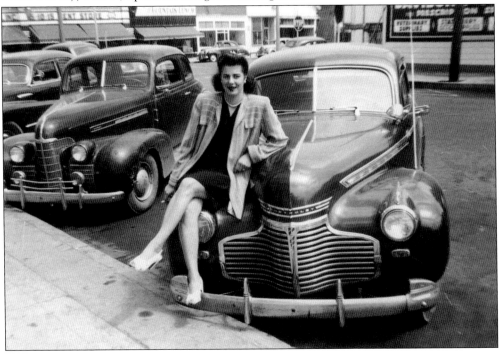

Three

GOVERNMENT AND
DEVELOPMENT

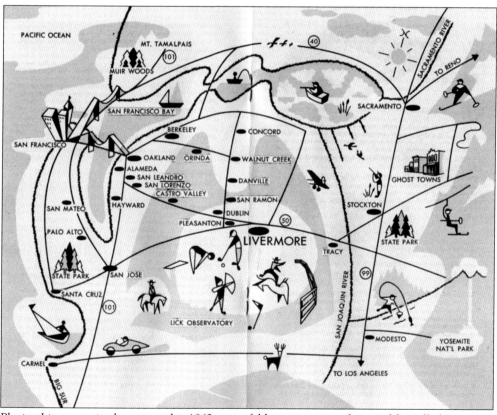

Placing Livermore in the center, this 1962 centerfold map was part of a pamphlet called *Livermore Facts*, cooperatively published by the Livermore Chamber of Commerce, Lawrence Radiation Laboratory, Sandia Corporation, General Electric Vallecitos Atomic Laboratory, Livermore Joint Union High School District, and the Livermore School District.

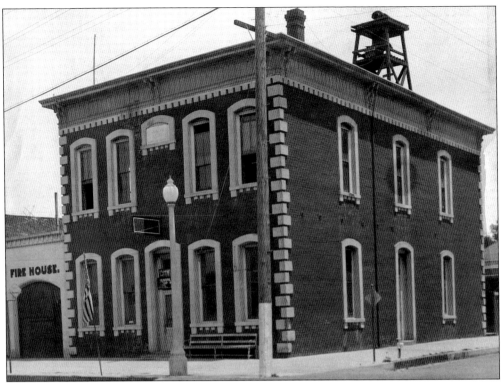

The c. 1925 photograph above shows Livermore's city hall. The city bought the building in 1905 with three installments of $1,000 to be paid to the Livermore Valley Bank over three years. The building had classic dentil and corbel details, deep-set, curved masonry window trim, and quoining. The structure on the roof housed a siren to call the volunteer firefighting force and a curfew bell. Below is an E.J. Lawless postcard photograph taken at the rededication of Livermore's city hall in February 1936. It was remodeled as part of a WPA project in the popular Art Deco style. Located on the southeast corner of First and McLeod Streets, the building served as the town hall till 1957. The police department also operated out of the building, and the jail was in the one-story building to the right.

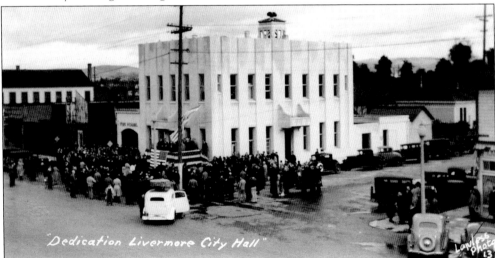

"Dedication Livermore City Hall"

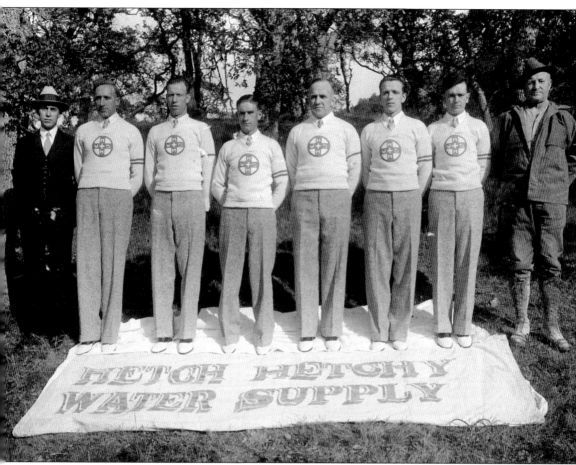

The Hetch Hetchy Aqueduct, begun in 1927, brought water from the Sierra Nevada to San Francisco. Some 2,000 men tunneled 28.5 miles through the Coast Range Mountains in two sections—25 miles from Tesla Portal to Alameda Creek, then 3.5 miles to Irvington Portal. Tesla Portal headquarters (1929) were at North L Street and Railroad Avenue. Supplies came in by rail for the five tunneling camps—Thomas, Mitchell, Mocho, Valley, and Indian Creek. In July 1930, when 12 men perished in Mitchell Shaft, the Hetch Hetchy Water Supply Company (HHWS) was exonerated in their deaths. A Hetch Hetchy Hospital was established in Livermore (L Street near Arroyo Del Valle) in September 1930. In October 1931, HHWS teams competed in the California Safety Society First Aid Competition at Hetch Hetchy Hospital. Members of the Mocho Camp Team, from left to right, are instructor Stanley M Jarrett, team captain Frank Holmes, James Daffer, John F White, H.H. Hammel, Hubert Hughes, Howard Kezar, and camp supervisor P.A. Peterson.

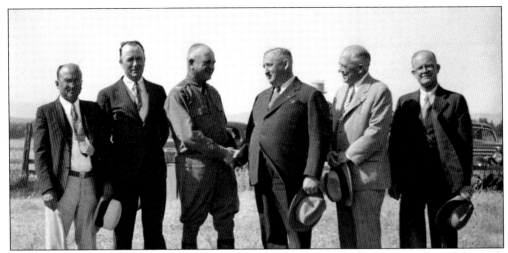

In this c. 1936 image, Livermore mayor George Tubbs meets with the commanders of the 30th Infantry Division when it camped out at the old rodeo grounds. Tubbs was mayor from 1935 to 1940, presiding over many of the city's WPA projects. He created "Tubbsville," a low-income housing settlement.

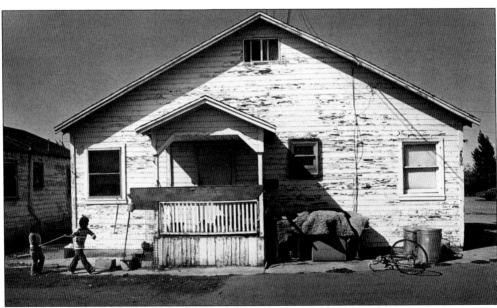

This house in Tubbsville, officially called Pacific Court, was located on the north side of Railroad Avenue between L and P Streets. These homes were salvaged from the abandoned mining town of Tesla in the early 1930s by George Tubbs, who saw the mining homes as a means of providing affordable housing during the Depression. The city razed Tubbsville in 1988.

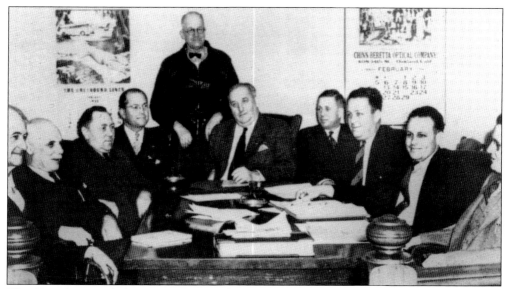

This 1940 photograph shows, from left to right, Elmer Still (city clerk), Sam Bothwell (councilman), Ernest Wente (councilman), F. Ray Hearn (treasurer), George Doten (chief of police), George Tubbs (councilman), Clark Clarke (city engineer), Harold Anderson (mayor), Louis Gardella (councilman, mayor 1950–1954), and Richard Callaghan (city attorney). Anderson was mayor from 1940 to 1950, serving through the end of the Great Depression, World War II, and the beginnings of postwar suburbanization. (Photograph by Elliot Dopking.)

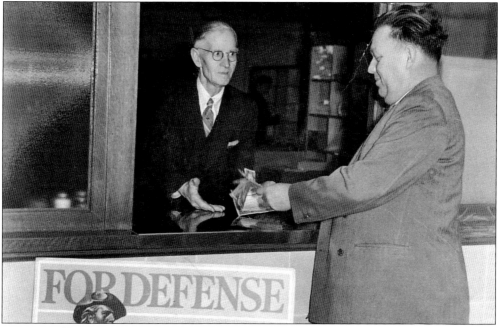

Mayor Harold Anderson purchases Livermore's first Defense Bond from postmaster W.R. McKinnon in 1941 at the beginning of World War II. In the Sixth Bond Campaign (1944), Livermore raised $481,103.25. J.S. Concannon was given special recognition as the state chairman of the Winemakers War Loan Campaign, which raised $7.5 million. The 1930s post office (206 South J Street) was converted into a USO center and held weekly events.

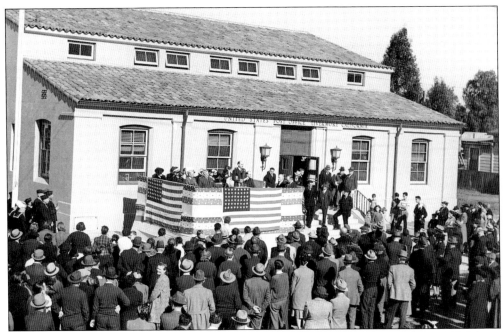

The Livermore Post Office on South Livermore Avenue was dedicated March 2, 1940. Mayor George Tubbs made opening remarks. Oakland Superior Court judge S. Victor Wagler is pictured giving the dedication address. Approved by an act of Congress and built at an expense of $54,729, it was the first US post office in Livermore. The building was designated a nuclear fallout shelter in the 1950s.

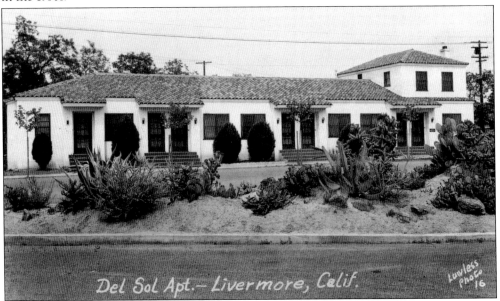

Del Sol Apt. – Livermore, Calif.

A Livermore cactus garden is pictured about 1935 on this Lawless Drug postcard. Created in 1934 by volunteer John Ferrario, it flourished for 31 years. Then in 1965, the Rotary Club spent $1,200 to install lawn, trees, and pathways. The Del Sol Apartments appear in the background on the east side of South Livermore between Fifth and H Streets. In 1931, Del Sol was owned by Lona Lincoln, who sold the property to Mr. and Mrs. Roy Anderson in 1943.

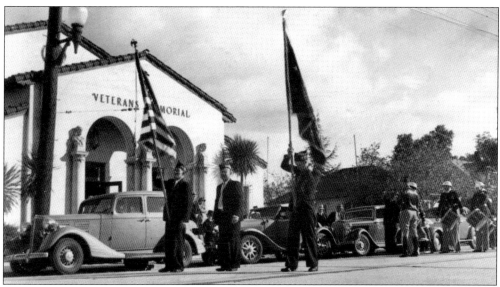

A veterans parade passes the Veterans Memorial Building at 522 South L Street. The Veterans Memorial Building was dedicated on August 23, 1931, with an opening address by Alameda County supervisor Ralph Richmond. That evening, a ball was held with both modern and old-time music provided by Christensen's Orchestra. Designed by Livermore native and architect Henry Meyers, the Spanish Revival building has a lobby leading to a 50-by-75-foot auditorium, a lodge room, men's and women's club rooms, and a kitchen. The auditorium was equipped with a projection booth and a raised stage. Below, Livermore post American Legion veterans plant a tree outside the Veterans Memorial Building as a memorial to Livermore Valley residents who served during World War II (1946). From left to right are Robert White, D.A. Gildersleeve, Carl Addleman, Leo Fehrenbach, Livermore post commander J.J. Kelly, O.A. Page, S.E. Smith, and W. Gatzmer Wagoner.

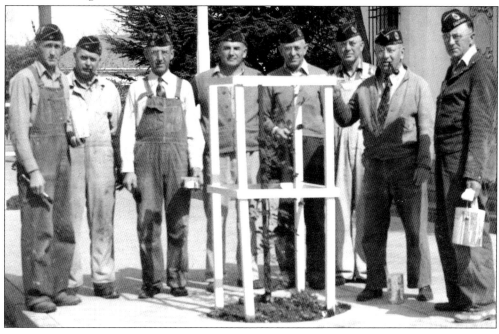

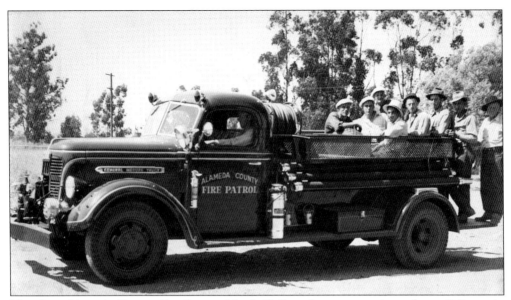

Men from Alameda County Fire Station No. 8, College Avenue, are pictured near P Street in this 1938 Elliott Dopking photograph. From left to right are Gene Flynn (behind the wheel) Jack Watt, Dan Hansen, Charles Watt, Steve Robles, Creighton Evans, Wesley Olsen, Francis Rochin, and Dan Fuson. Station No. 8 firefighters responded locally and as far as Mount Diablo. Fire warden James McGlinchey served from 1937 until 1965. The station was dedicated to his father, John McGlinchey, in 1950. (Elliott Dopking.)

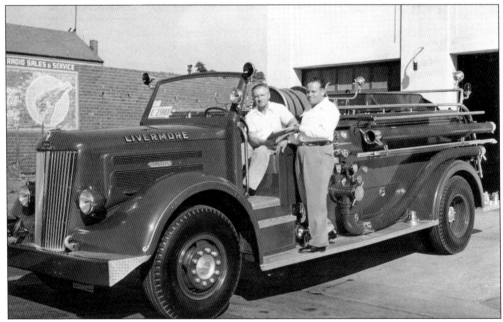

Livermore's fire chief Al Bonne and former mayor Louis Gardella pose for a 1956 photograph on the 500-gallon 1950 White/Van Pelt 750-gallons-per-minute pumper at the old city hall at McLeod and First Streets. This was the city's only firehouse until 1964. Bonne retired a year after this photograph was taken, having served a total of 10 years. Gardella served as Livermore's mayor from 1950 until 1954.

When former chief Al Bonne retired (1957), Jack Baird (pictured) was promoted to Livermore fire chief and served until 1980. Baird transformed the fire department from a mostly volunteer force into a full-time professional fire company. Baird attended Livermore High School and became president of the local 4-H and a member of the local Red Cross board.

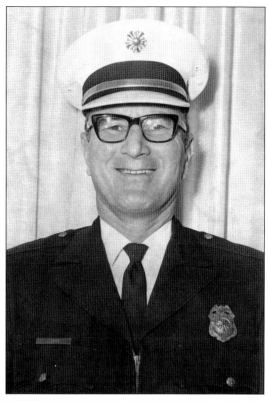

Two of the city's fire trucks are visible outside city hall about 1950. From left to right are the 1950s White/Van Pelt and 1940s GMC. On the left, with the Coca-Cola sign, is the 1927 Lydiksen Building. The Livermore Heritage Guild has lovingly restored the city's 1915-era Model T Ford fire car, 1920 Seagrave, and 1944 Mack fire engines. They are common sights in community parades and events.

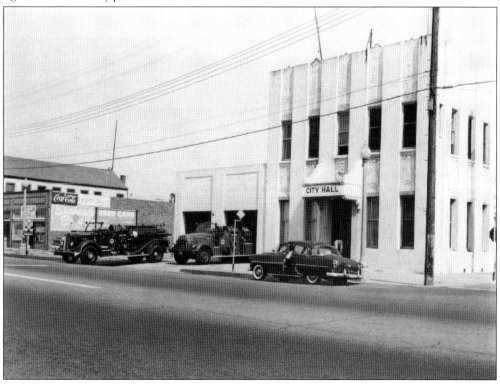

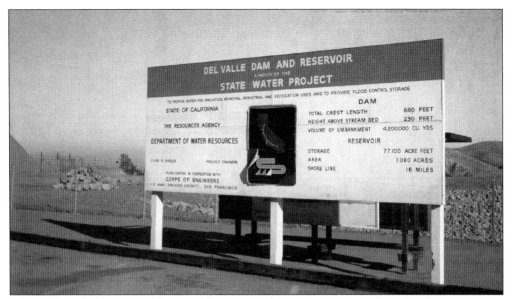

The earth embankment–style Del Valle Dam and Reservoir were built under the supervision of the US Army Corps of Engineers at a cost of $17 million starting in 1967. The sign at the entrance to the project details the size and capacity of the dam. The dam is located five miles south of the city of Livermore.

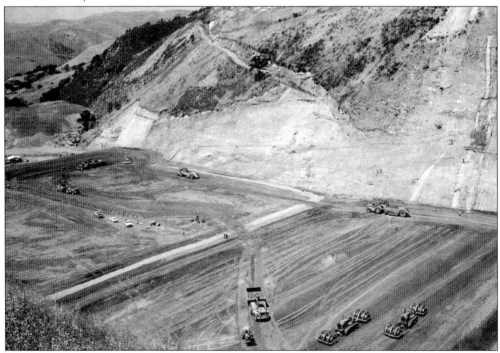

Earthmoving equipment of the Green Construction Company (Des Moines) and Winston Brothers (Minneapolis) moved four million cubic yards of dirt to form the dam's shape, shown here in 1967. The land had been zoned an Alameda County watershed district in 1913, and the project intermittently surfaced as early as 1939, but it was not until 1966 that Congress passed the funding bill to build the dam.

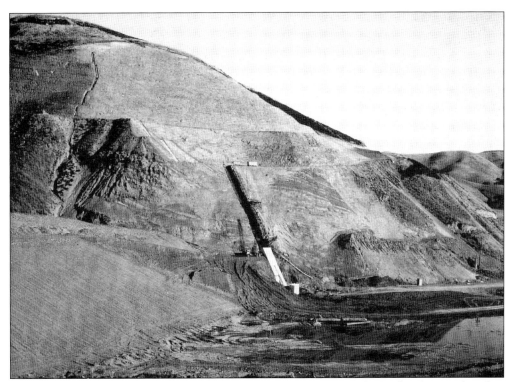

Concrete support is being formed for Del Valle Dam in 1967. Built for flood control and to secure a stable water supply for the expanding suburbs, the dam is part of the East Bay Regional Park system.

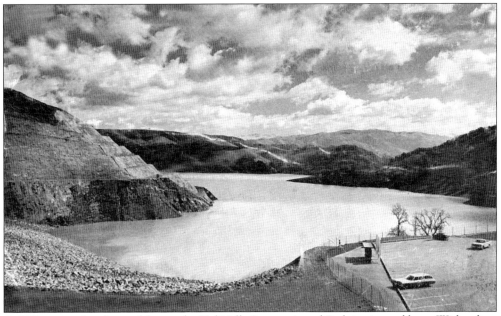

A 1969 promotional pamphlet on the Del Valle Reservoir and Park is pictured here. With a five-mile-long lake, the site features campgrounds and is a popular spot for boaters, fishermen, hikers, horseback riders, picnickers, and swimmers.

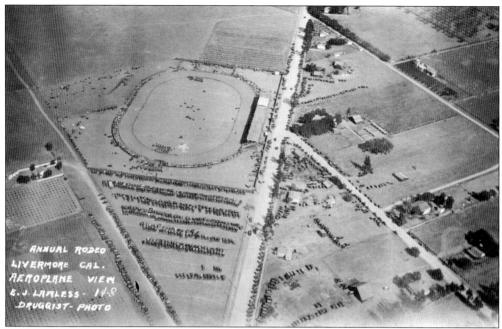

The old rodeo grounds are pictured about 1935. The city condemned the grandstands as unsafe in 1959, effectively canceling that year's rodeo. In what was called "The Trade," the Livermore Stockmen's Association gave the 40-plus acres to the city and received rights to use the new stadium, built in 1968 at Robertson Park. In this image, South Livermore Avenue cuts diagonally south to north. The road to the left is Pacific Avenue.

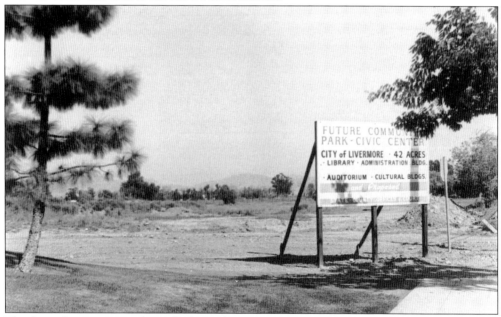

The Civic Center site was formerly the Rodeo Grounds until the Stockman's Association traded the land to the city. The focal point of the new site was a library, built with money raised by a 1964 bond measure. The site now contains the Civic Administration Building, city hall, the police department, "The Barn" and MultiService Center, Sunken Gardens, and Gardella Green.

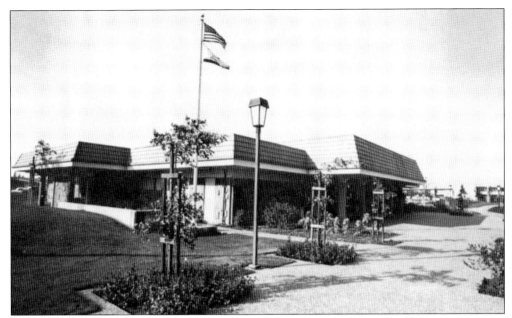

The 1966 library at the Civic Center is pictured here. Construction on this library began in December 1965; it opened 10 months later. The library, by architect Burns Cadwalader, cost about $500,000 to build and featured a smoking lounge, a community meeting room, and air-conditioning. By 1967, the library was lending 270,000 books to the booming population. The Civic Center Library was built to replace the Carnegie library, which had been in use since 1911.

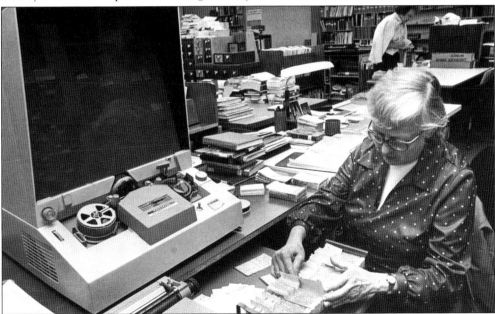

Pictured is Freddie Wondolonski, a Livermore Public Library volunteer. During the 1960s and 1970s, Livermore's public services, including the library, expanded to accommodate the growing community. Volunteers like Freddie, as well as the library's dedicated staff, were responsible for the circulation of over 60,000 books, records, and even eight-millimeter films in the late 1960s and early 1970s. The 1966 Civic Center Library was used until 2003.

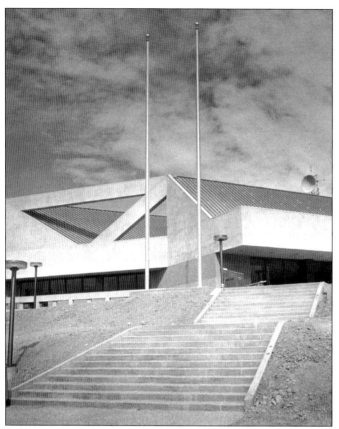

The Civic Administration Building, seen shortly after construction in 1979, was built over the city's existing 1974 police department. Designed by architect Peter Scott of Berkeley, the project had a number of stops and starts. The final cost of the center was $1.434 million.

City hall is pictured in November 1963 with the flag at half-mast following the assassination of Pres. John F. Kennedy. The Bank of Italy Building served as city hall from 1957 to 1979.

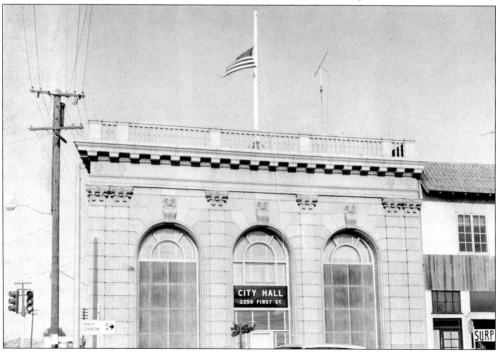

This 1972 Measure "B" flyer was created by Save All Valley Environments Incorporated (SAVE), led by many employees of Livermore's research laboratories who gathered 5,700 signatures to get "B" on the ballot. SAVE advocated slow growth and fought development by calling attention to the problems facing other cities. Late-1960s developments, such as Somerset Homes near Highway 50, brought suburbanites who were chiefly commuters.

Facing west, this c. 1963 aerial view of Livermore shows an increase in housing developments. East Avenue divides the image, with the 1950 Jensen Development laid out in a square pattern on the right and East Avenue School and the Independent Order of Odd Fellows (IOOF) cemetery (now known as Memory Gardens) on the left.

SAVE = "B"

Run away growth leads to run away TAXES.
Measure "B" is a positive force insuring that
growth pays for itself.

Run away growth has caused perpetual school crowding.
Measure "B" does away with endless double sessions
and over crowded high schools.

Run away growth threatens you with water rationing
this summer.
Measure "B" prevents future water rationing.

Measure "B" means no sudden catastrophes such as
the sewer crises in Pleasanton and Dublin which
has stopped all growth including industrial and
commercial.

Measure "B" applies only to new dwelling units.
It will not affect your home or any improvements
you plan.

Pressure groups are fighting only measure "B".
Their money would be better spent to help provide
schools.

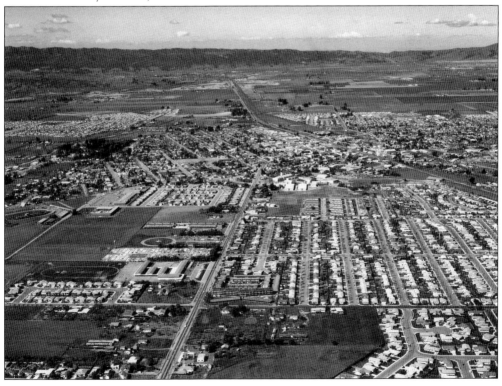

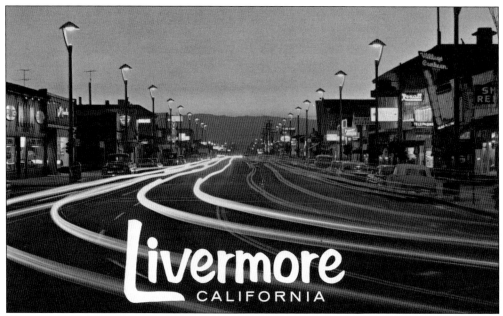

This is a 1965 Livermore Chamber of Commerce catalog cover by Charles F. Holbrook. The catalog advertised Livermore as a bedroom community linked to Oakland and San Francisco via I-580. The LIvermore Chamber of Commerce boasted that the city's housing had jumped 800 percent between 1940 and 1964. The 1965 population was 25,000, compared to less than 3,000 only 15 years earlier. The unique streetlights were generally replaced, but several remain along First Street.

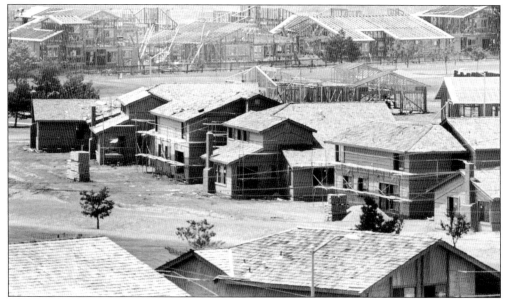

This late-1960s photograph shows more homes under construction and echoes the growth of suburban development that Bill Owens would make famous in his book *Suburbia*. He worked as a photographer for the *Independent*, the local newspaper. A 1964 Livermore Chamber of Commerce brochure sums up the city's transformation: "[Livermore's] future collided head-on with the past, and a way of life was caught in the middle."

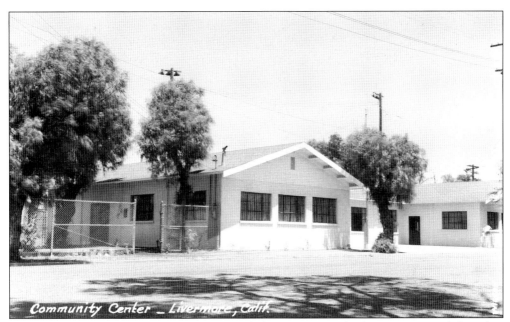

Samuel Bothwell Recreation Center, pictured about 1950, was built in 1949 at Eighth and H Streets. Originally the Livermore Community Center, it was renamed by LARPD in 1965 to honor Bothwell's civic contributions. Bothwell, a local builder and a city councilman from 1932 to 1940, managed many of Livermore's WPA projects, was president of the ration board during World War II, and oversaw the center's construction. He died in 1952.

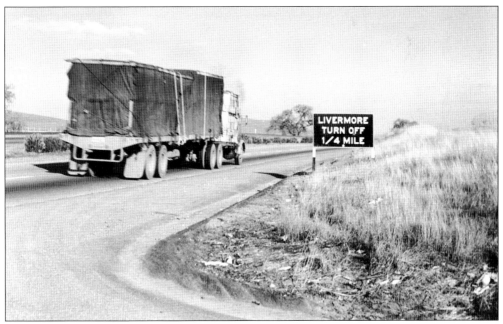

Before giving way to Interstate 580, Highway 50 linked Livermore to the East Bay and the Central Valley. Originally a four-lane road, it swelled to eight lanes. By 1971, Interstate 580 was connected to Interstate 680. I-580 was the essential piece of infrastructure that transformed Livermore into a bedroom community for commuters.

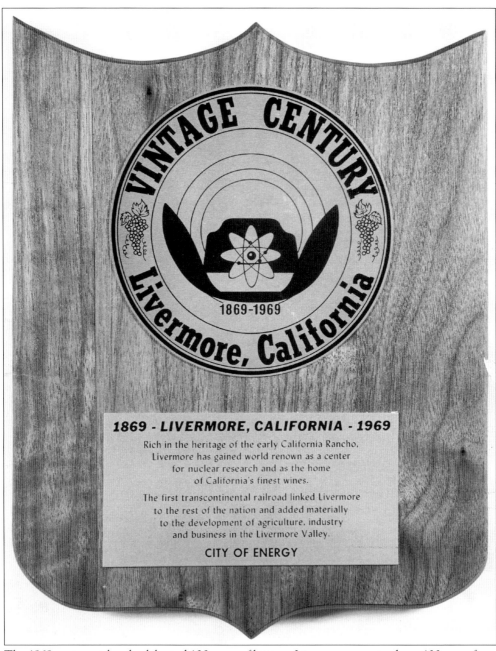

VINTAGE CENTURY
Livermore, California
1869-1969

1869 - LIVERMORE, CALIFORNIA - 1969

Rich in the heritage of the early California Rancho,
Livermore has gained world renown as a center
for nuclear research and as the home
of California's finest wines.

The first transcontinental railroad linked Livermore
to the rest of the nation and added materially
to the development of agriculture, industry
and business in the Livermore Valley.

CITY OF ENERGY

The 1969 centennial seal celebrated 100 years of history. Livermore grew in those 100 years from a town of about 830 to almost 40,000. This plaque honors Livermore's heritage while embracing the future as the "City of Energy." The seal was designed by artist and Sandia employee Ed Watchempino. His work was used on city stationery, bumper stickers, and even beer mugs commemorating the city's milestone.

Four

Civic Growth

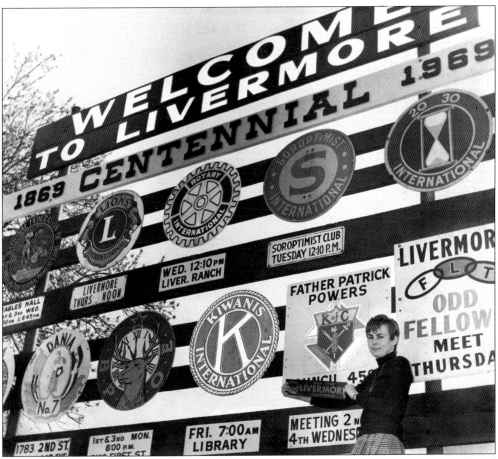

Livermore's civic institutions and fraternal organizations have been instrumental in its cultural growth. This welcome sign, constructed for the 1969 centennial, hints at the over 100 civic and service clubs that existed at the time, many with roots from the turn of the century and still thriving today. They reveal a proactive community with a commitment to a shared future.

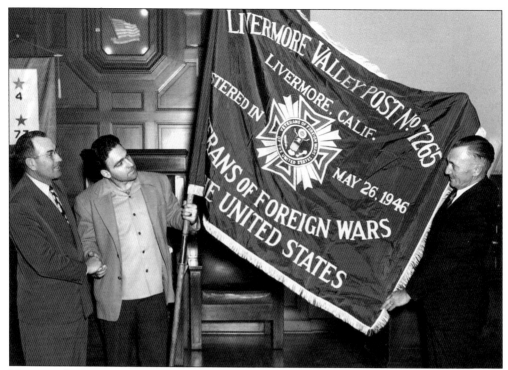

Veterans of Foreign Wars members inspect the banner of their new organization. From left to right are Chester Stanley, Chi Vukota, and unidentified. Livermore Valley Post No. 7265, Veterans of Foreign Wars, was organized in May 1946. With an initial roster of 83 members including many prominent Livermore residents, it elected Francis W. Vukota as commander.

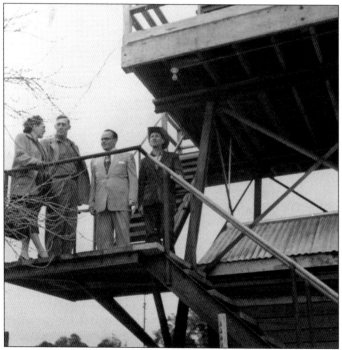

Livermore's enemy aircraft observation tower, built January 1953, was located in the city corporation yard on Railroad Avenue and was staffed by volunteers 24 hours a day. Construction was managed by local contractors Roy Jensen and Sam Bothwell, using volunteer labor and steel donated from Henry Kaiser. Pictured from left to right are Mrs. Lawrence McClaskey, councilman B.F. Carter, Mayor Louis Gardella, and post supervisor Sterling Bosley.

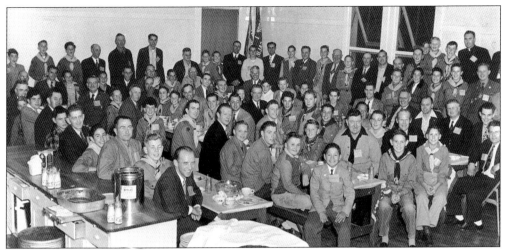

Scouting has played a prominent role in the lives of many young men living in Livermore since the founding of the first troop in 1910. This earliest local Scout troop languished, and what is known as Livermore Troop No. 1 was founded in 1921 by E.J. Lawless. The Scouts in this 1947 photograph would have enjoyed the wilderness camp on Mines Road built on 686 acres donated in 1944 by Auto Mechanics Union of Oakland in support of Bay Area youth.

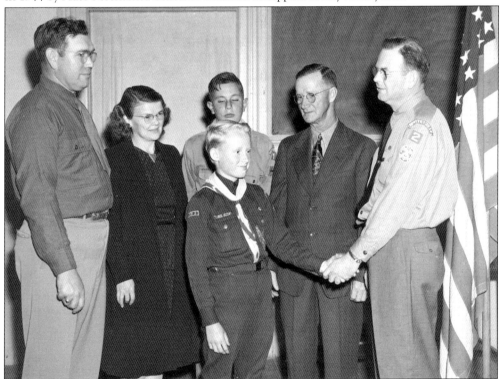

Robert Guthrie is being congratulated by Cub Scout pack leader Leo Callaghan (Livermore Troop No. 2) for advancing to Boy Scout in this 1946 ceremony. Surrounding him are, from left to right, Jack Wallace (Cub pack leader), den mother Mrs. B.S. Horton, assistant den chief Billy Beckowitz, and Robert's father, O.F. Guthrie. Boy Scouts played a crucial role in heading scrap drives during World War II.

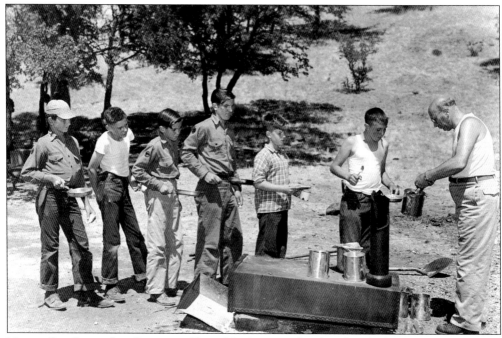

Hungry Boy Scouts from Livermore Troop No. 1 wait in the chow line for hot meals in 1955. The Boy Scouts' Los Mochos Wilderness Camp at Sweet Water Springs, founded in 1944 and still in existence today as Rancho Los Mochos, gives Scouts a camping and wilderness experience. Many Scout badges are earned in Livermore's southern hills. Pictured from left to right are Jerry Jensen, Bob Streitz, Billy Smith, Jimmy Smith, Roy Creager, Billy Berkowitz, and Scoutmaster Harry Berkowitz.

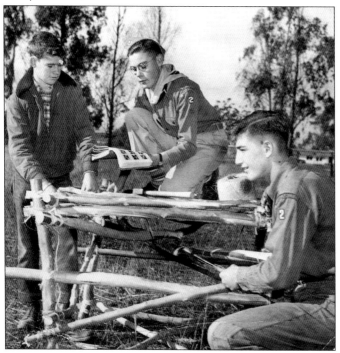

Boy Scouts from Livermore Troop No. 2 put their scouting knowledge to work at the Los Mochos camp around 1945. In addition to earning badges, scouts also learned the importance of teamwork on their retreats to Los Mochos.

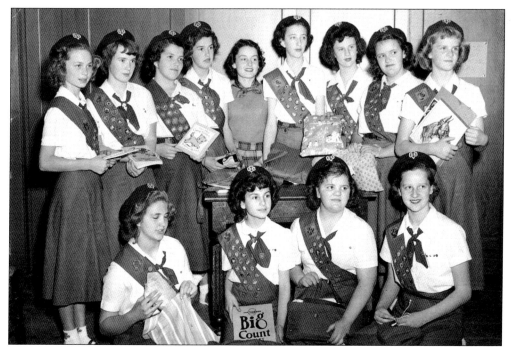

As part of a national Girl Scouts program, Schoolmates Overseas, Livermore Troop No. 3 poses with assembled school kits in a 1950 fundraising campaign. The Girl Scouts formed in Livermore in 1939 and are still active today. From left to right are (first row) Margaret Owens, Carol Ann Lewis, Mary Greene, and Anna Walsted; (second row) Maxine Nissen, Jean Armstrong, Audrey Westfall, Kay Wissler, Serena Webb, Rene Viale, Edith Raboli, Dorothy Greene, and Patricia Holm.

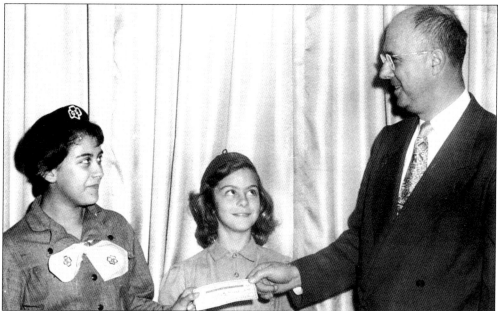

Delphine Bankhead (left) and Judy Wood of Del Valle Girl Scout Council pose for a photograph with Andrew Perry Jr., president of Livermore Valley Community Chest, during a 1952 award ceremony.

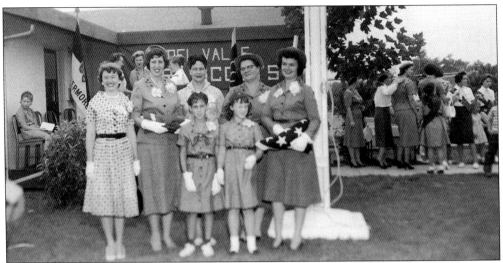

This flagpole dedication was held in September 1960 at Del Valle Girl Scout House in Paul E. Dolan Park (Dolan founded St. Paul's Hospital) at 2800 Ladd Avenue. Pacific Telephone and Telegraph donated the pole, and Mr. and Mrs. Maitland R. Henry donated the flag in memory of daughter Jean Henry Atkin, a member of Livermore's first Girl Scout troop. From left to right are (first row) Shirley Evans and Gayle Koopman; (second row) Betty Byer Beaudet, Mildred Lenn Evans, unidentified, Scout leader Edith Wood, and Tillie Anderson Koopman.

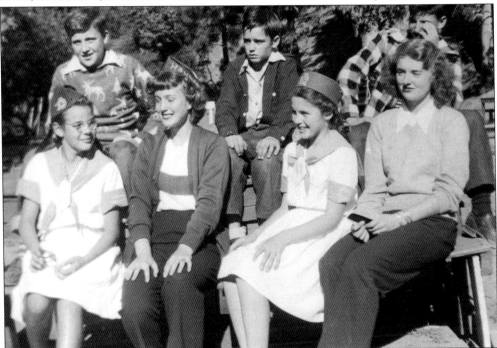

The 1946 winners of the 4-H (Head, Heart, Hands, and Health) Achievement Awards at Hayward Memorial Park are pictured here. From left to right are (first row) Betty Koze, Elaine Brown, Mary Ann Ginger, and Betty Ralph; (second row) Billy Ralph, Terry Rooney, and Don Frick, all from Livermore. Billy won the farm bureau's $50 first place prize and used the money to purchase three ewes.

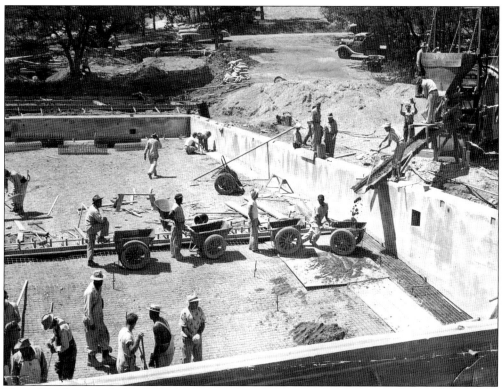

This 1950 photograph shows the construction of the pool at the Boy Scout Rancho Los Mochos camp off of Mines Road, 19 miles south of Livermore. Forty-five men from the Local Cement Finishers Union No. 594 volunteered their time to build the 40-by-105-foot pool.

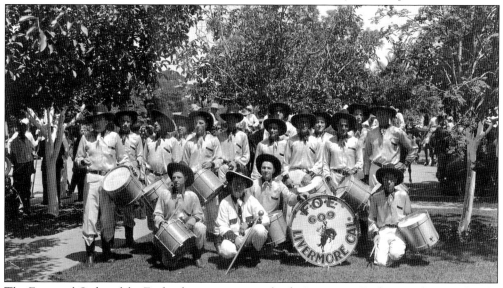

The Fraternal Order of the Eagles drum corps poses for the Livermore Rodeo Parade around 1950. Founded in 1904, the Livermore Aerie No. 609 has participated in numerous community events. In 1945, the Eagles had 700 members. They raised $6,000 to build a hall at 527 Livermore Avenue that opened August 1950. A women's auxiliary was also formed that year.

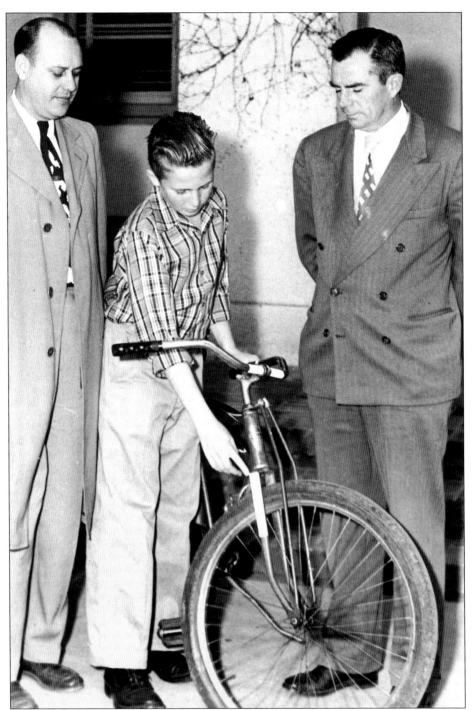

The 20-30 Club, a national men's service organization, founded a Livermore branch in 1947. Raising funds for Valley Memorial Hospital became its main focus during the 1950s. Members of the 1955 Bicycle Project are, from left to right, Joe Mitchell, an unidentified boy, and Carson Hussey (project lead). To raise safety awareness, 20 to 30 members visited local schools and placed reflective red tape on children's bicycles.

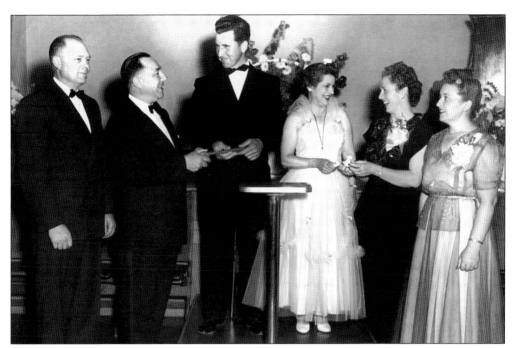

The Fraternal Order of the Eagle aerie (lodge) installs new officers for the Eagles and the Women's Auxiliary in a 1952 ceremony. From left to right are Vernon Olson, C.J. Francisco, new president William Silva, new president Roberta White, Mrs. C.J. Francisco, and Mrs. Manuel Medeiros. The aerie is still active in the community and meets in the same 1950s clubhouse on Livermore Avenue.

The Independent Order of Odd Fellows (IOOF) and women's Rebekah Lodge No. 154 have been stable Livermore civic organizations. Founded in 1873, IOOF built Livermore's first fraternal lodge at 2160 First Street, and the group is still active today. This 1947 photograph shows the passing of the gavel (right to left) to new officers. Mrs. Harold Nylen passes her gavel to Mrs. A.R. Rettig; Harold Nylen passes his to Oris Engblom.

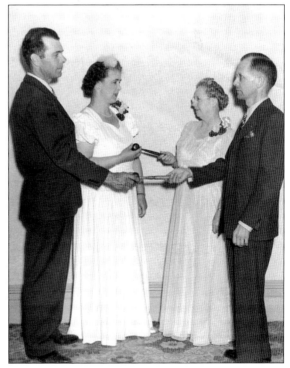

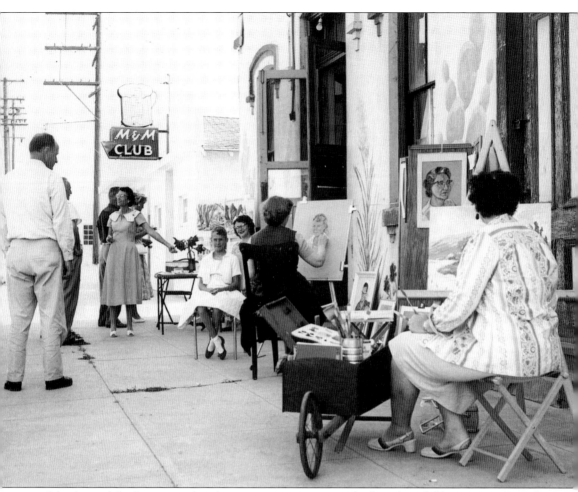

Members of the Livermore Art Association painting outside their first clubhouse at 141 North Livermore Avenue are pictured in 1957. Since 1974, the art association and the Livermore Heritage Guild have shared the upper floor of the Carnegie library building. Artwork is on display and for sale. The group sponsors yearly events and is open to all.

Five

HEALTH CARE

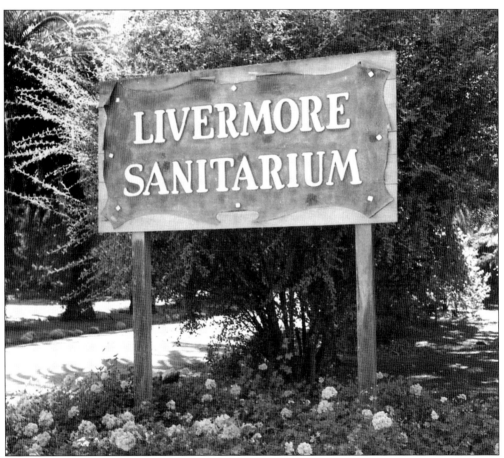

In 1931, six Livermore health facilities were placed on an accredited register of American Medical Association–approved hospitals. Those listed were the Arroyo Del Valle Sanatorium, Hetch Hetchy Hospital, Judson Hospital, St. Paul's Hospital, Livermore Sanitarium, and US Veterans Hospital. The dry, temperate climate and clean-air country location were seen as beneficial to the treatment of tuberculosis. Livermore's chamber of commerce had a campaign slogan in the late 1920s through the 1930s, which claimed one could "Live Longer in Livermore."

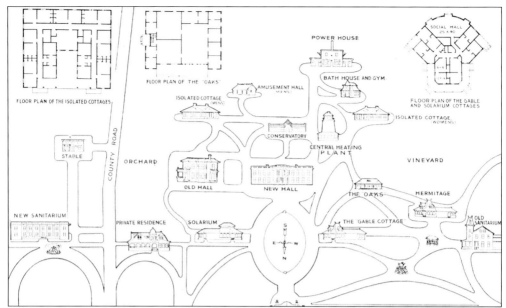

Renowned psychiatrist Dr. John Robertson purchased the Livermore Collegiate Institute building and William Mendenhall Mansion on the south side of College Avenue near Arroyo Road. (County Road in the map above), and founded a 120-patient psychiatric hospital in 1894. The facility expanded to provide general nursing care for patients suffering from "dyspepsia, nervous exhaustion, alcoholism and morphinism." An early advertisement for the Livermore Sanitarium is shown below. Through the postwar era, the sanitarium's facilities remained largely original, but by 1964, the number of patients was too small to sustain operations. New drugs for the treatment of mental illness were viewed as a positive alternative to institutional living. The grounds were beautifully landscaped to provide a peaceful, healing setting. The southeast corner of College Avenue and Arroyo Road still has the century-old palms and cedars. In the late 1970s, much of the land was sold for the construction of housing developments.

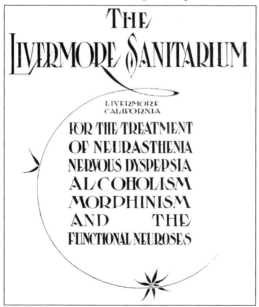

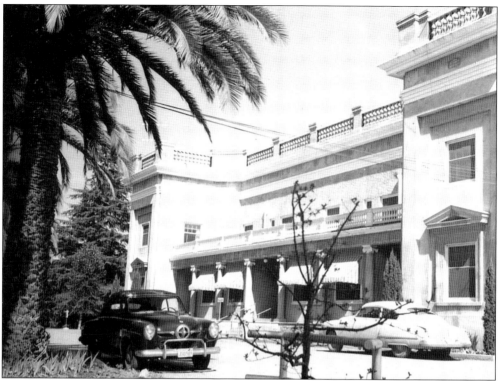

These c. 1954 views show the Hydropathic Building, listed as "New Sanitarium" on the layout map on the adjacent page. Built in 1909, at approximately 60-feet-by-100-feet in size, the building housed independent patients suffering from alcoholism or depression and who required only general supervision as they were not considered a threat to themselves or others. These patients could walk to downtown with a nurse. The Hydropathic Building housed doctors' offices, treatment rooms, a drug room, a lounge with a piano and four pool tables, a formal dining room, and the facility's main kitchen.

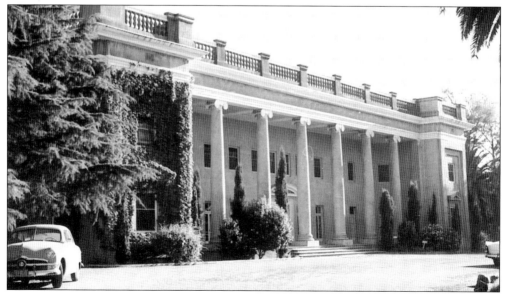

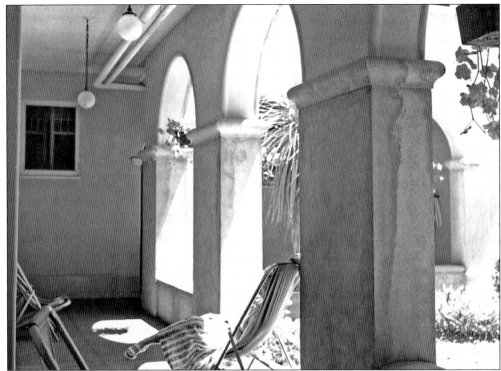

Above is a c. 1945 view of one of the sanitarium's many walkways. Dr. John Robinson believed that the open spaces and inviting grounds were an important part of treatment. The abundance of plants and open, airy windows resembles a beautiful country estate rather than an institution for the treatment of mental illness. The image below shows patients lounging on the lawn outside the gymnasium. In 1937, the sanitarium consisted of 140 acres, of which 20 were utilized for institution's buildings. There were 20 buildings in this period—10 for the care and treatment of patients. The sanitarium employed about 300 people. In addition to doctors and nurses, other employees included gardeners, painters, carpenters, electricians, launderers, cooks, farmers, and housekeepers. The sanitarium raised its own vegetables, chickens, eggs, beef, and pork.

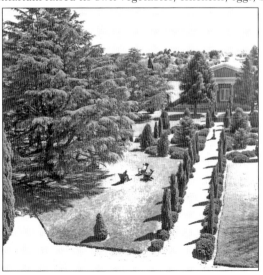

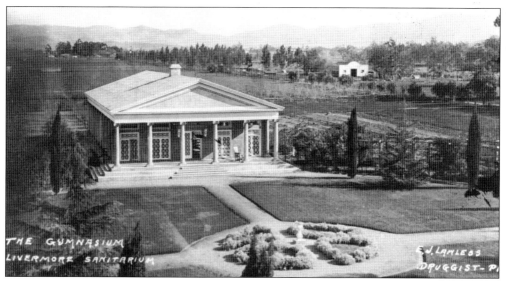

The gymnasium, pictured above in a c. 1935 Lawless Drug postcard, was an essential component of the Livermore Sanitarium's treatment regimen. Daily calisthenic classes were held in the gym as cited in Dr. C.W. Mack's *Therapeutic Application of Physical Education*. Designed to encourage exercise and relaxation for patients, the building was modeled on the Parthenon and fits with the grand architectural style of the turn of the century. Below is a c. 1945 photograph of the covered pool that was also housed within the gymnasium. Dr. John Robinson Jr. (the founder's son) worked at the sanitarium until he retired in 1954.

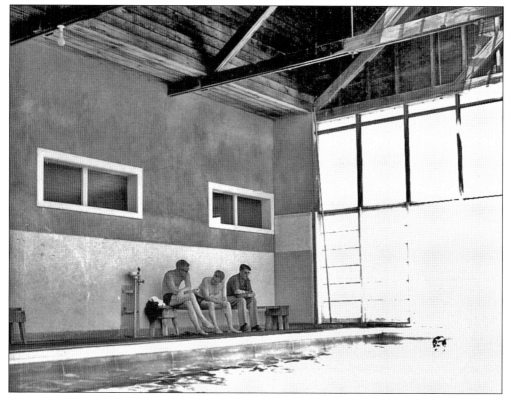

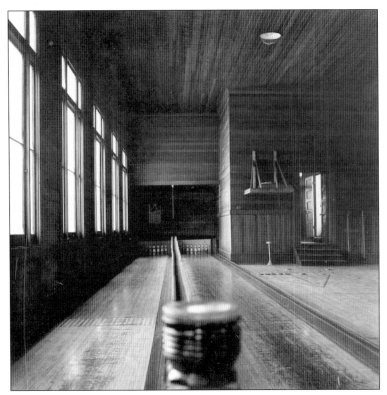

Recreation and relaxation were deemed essential to treatment. This is a c. 1945 photograph of the sanitarium's gymnasium, showing that the patients had access to a two-lane bowling alley and shuffleboard. This building was torn down in 1965. Volleyball, tennis, croquet, and miniature golf were also available to patients.

An empty smoking lounge within the Hydropathic Building is pictured about 1960. The Livermore Sanitarium announced its closing in August 1964. Decline in patient submittals, changing methods that included newer outpatient drug therapies, and the establishment of psychiatric wards in general hospitals were cited as causes. Property east of the Hydropathic Building and the former poultry yard was sold for residential development in the late 1950s and early 1960s.

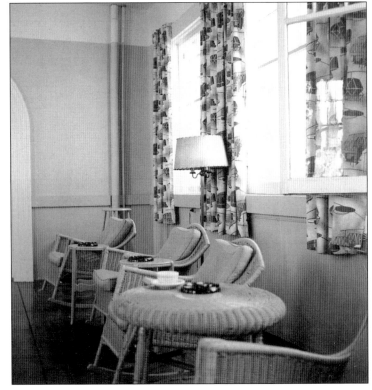

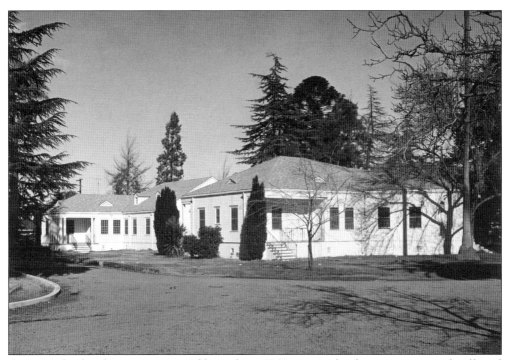

A group of isolated cottages, pictured here about 1960, was used to house more severely affected patients. By 1967, most of the sanitarium's buildings had been demolished. New housing developments such as Chateau Park and Forest Glade have been constructed on the land as part of Livermore's postwar growth and transition into a suburban community.

A nurse at the sanitarium prepares medication for patients about 1940. In addition to medication, the sanitarium emphasized environment and serenity as crucial parts of the patient's treatment. Livermore's sanitarium was a stark contrast to many East Coast hospital-style institutions. The sanitarium seemed as much a community as a psychiatric ward. Most of the medical staff lived on the grounds.

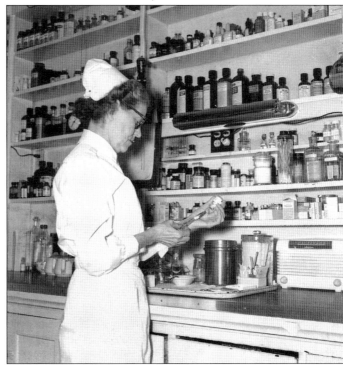

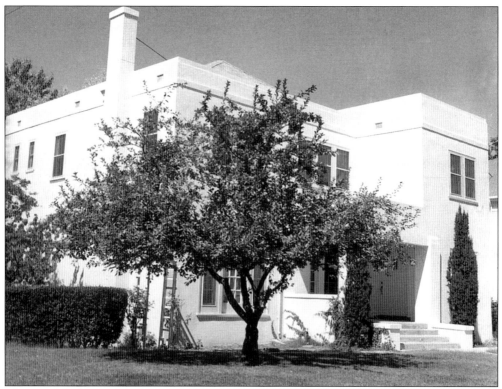

This c. 1940 photograph shows Dr. Clifford W. Mack's house, which he shared with his family. Dr. Mack was the superintendent of the Livermore Sanitarium from 1928 to 1948. The home is still located at 955 South L Street.

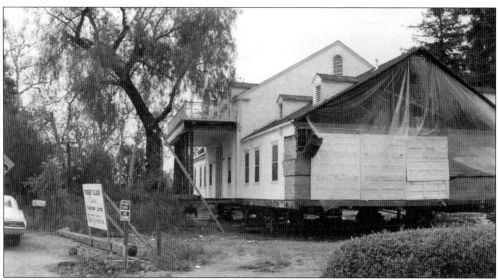

This sanitarium building, shown in 1979, was the middle section of the ward known as "The Gables." It housed women patients. In 1979, the house was purchased by Barbara and Lee Savoy, who moved it from its original location to its present location at 989 South L Street to serve as their private residence.

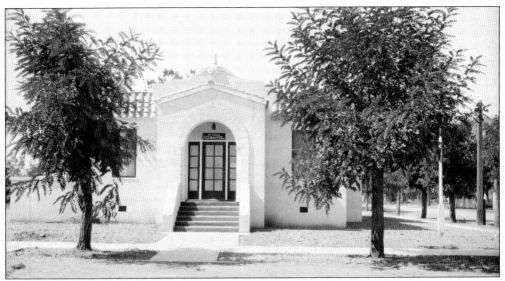

St. Paul's Hospital is pictured about 1935. Opened in June 1927 by Dr. Paul E. Dolan as a modern hospital on the southwest corner of Eighth and South J Streets, St. Paul's was originally a 46-by-96-foot Spanish Revival structure. The architect was A.T. Coffey; the building contractor, Nels Jensen. The hospital had private rooms, a ward for 11, and a partial basement. By the end of 1940, the hospital had doubled its occupancy to 24 beds via the addition of two new wings and had a maternity ward with air-conditioning and incubation units for premature births. It had the only emergency room between Stockton and Oakland. Dr. Dolan sold the hospital to Dr. Raymond Owens and Elsie Rivinius in 1951. The Valley Memorial Hospital Board purchased the facility in 1966 for $95,000. It is currently an assisted living center nestled in the "old South Side" neighborhood.

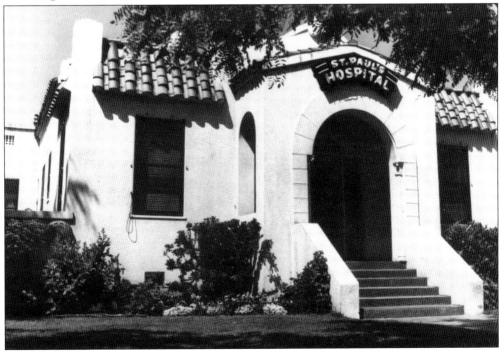

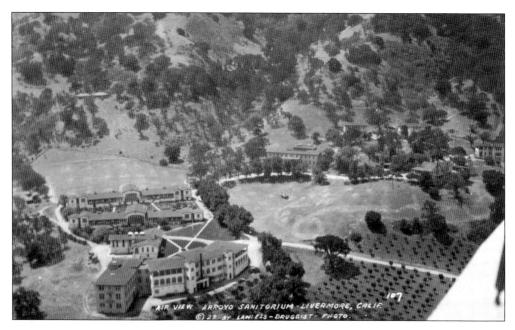

Two aerial views show the Arroyo Del Valle Sanatorium—a c. 1930 Lawless Drug photograph above and a c. 1935 image below. In February 1918, Alameda County opened a hospital facility for the treatment of tuberculosis (TB) in the foothills south of Livermore along the Arroyo Del Valle. The dry, mild climate was believed to be beneficial for TB patients. More than 10,000 patients were treated at the facility until it closed in 1960. TB is primarily a disease of the lungs and is considered highly contagious. Patients were isolated in wards, and visitors were brought in by bus. Del Valle Ranch, per a November 1937 reprint of *The Survey of Arroyo Sanatorium and Del Valle Farm as a Community*, was established as a preventorium, a place where undernourished and frail children could be prevented from developing TB, through a wholesome life with proper rest.

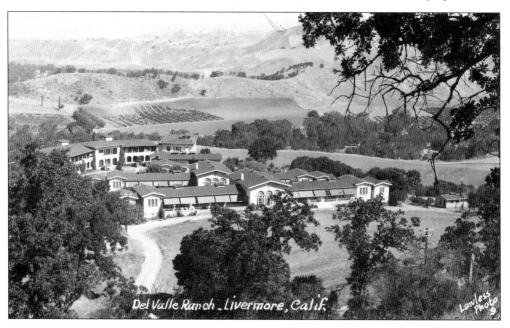

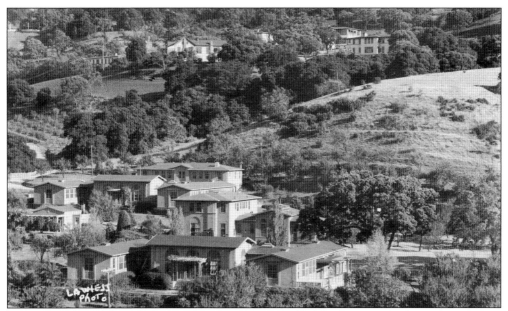

The Arroyo Del Valle Sanatorium is pictured above and below about 1935. The sanatorium was situated on 195 acres of land and was a self-sufficient center. The facilities included a fire station, dormitories for employees, an incinerator, and dietary kitchen. The site cost about $400,000 a year to operate in the late 1950s. Patients who were almost well enough for discharge had access to recreation rooms. A centralized radio station was provided; patients could listen by using bedside headphones. The sanatorium provided a weekly article in the *Livermore Herald* describing happenings at the hospital. Internally, the Arroyo had its own newspaper originally called the *Stethoscope*, later renamed the *Arroyan*.

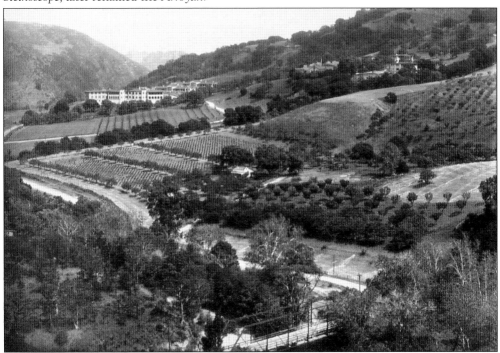

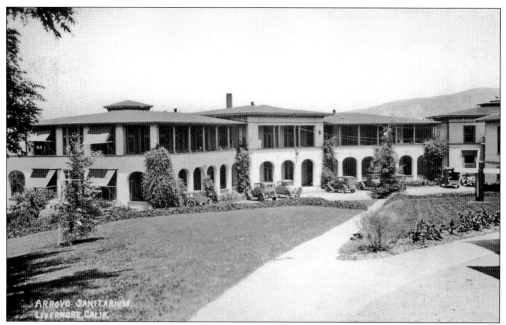

A convalescent ward is pictured here in the late 1920s. Women lived on the second floor and men on the first. Early TB treatments included lobectomy, removing a lung lobe; pneumothorax, or plombage, collapsing an infected lung to "rest" it and allow lesions to heal; or pneumonectomy, removing an entire lung. Better drug therapies—streptomycin in 1944 and isoniazid in 1952—made surgical treatments obsolete. Additionally, vaccination was widely employed following World War II.

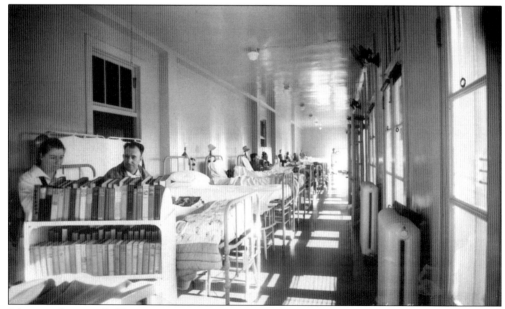

Librarian Lenora C. Hering visits patient Leonard C. Pillsbury in a Veterans Hospital ward in 1936. Patients were kept in bed, only sitting up to eat, in the early stages of recovery.

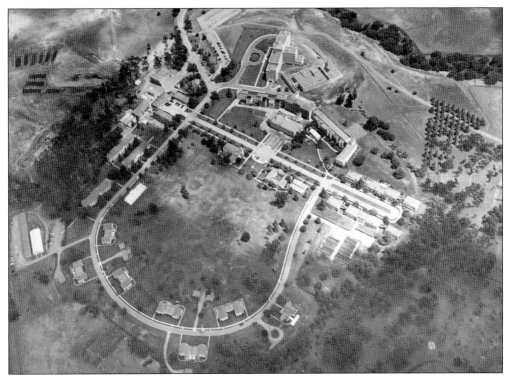

Above, an aerial photograph shows Livermore's US Veterans Administration (VA) Hospital about 1970. Dedicated in 1925 to provide tuberculosis treatment for veterans, the facility's mission shifted to include general medical, dental, surgical, and psychological care in the late 1950s. The VA Hospital was placed on 235 acres of land once part of the Cresta Blanca Vineyards. Dr. Frank B. Brewer was hospital director from 1929 to 1941. Dr. Ralph Newton worked there between 1945 and 1974. A third bout of tuberculosis in 1960 caused him to become a patient among his patients for 18 months. Dr. Newton and his wife, Janet, were founding members of the Livermore Heritage Guild and the Livermore Symphony Guild. The Lawless Drug photograph below shows the hospital about 1935. The main administrative and patient building is to the far right.

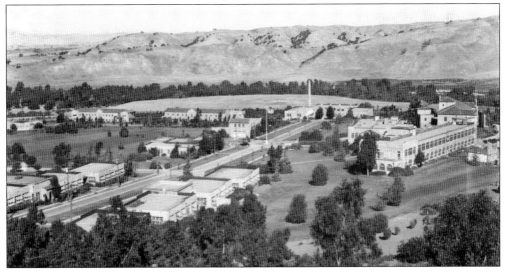

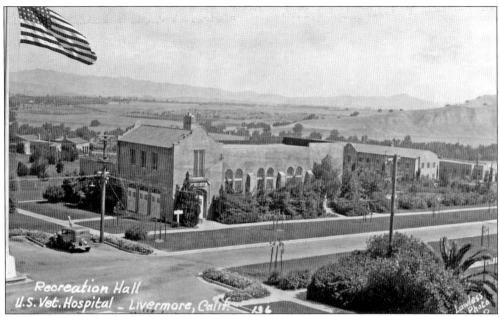

This Lawless Drug photograph shows the VA Hospital Recreation Hall about 1935. Patients could participate in recreational activities such as movies, parties, and clubs (including photography, puzzle, pottery, glee, drama, and bowling). The Recreation Hall had meeting rooms and an auditorium. The facility had its own radio station, KLVII, and library. In the 1930s and 1940s, the *Livermore Herald* published weekly news from the hospital in a column called Cresta Blanca News.

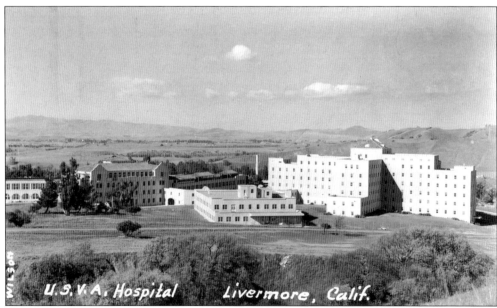

The Veterans Hospital is pictured here about 1950. The original complex had 24 buildings, including an infirmary, cottages, heating plant, laundry, shops, warehouses, post office, canteen, and staff quarters. The administration building is on the left; wings were added starting in the late 1930s. Building 62 (far right) was constructed for $2 million in 1948 and brought the hospital to over 500 beds. By 1969, the Veterans Hospital was the largest orthopedic hospital in the Bay Area.

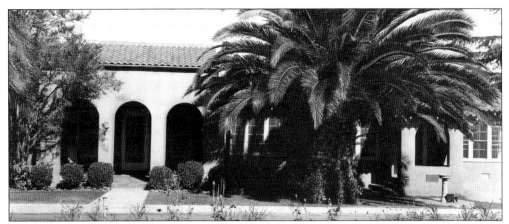

This c. 1935 Lawless Drug photograph shows the Veterans Hospital hostel and nursery. They provided a place for children to stay and be cared for while their relatives or parents visited patients. In 1958, the nursery cared for over 1,700 visiting children.

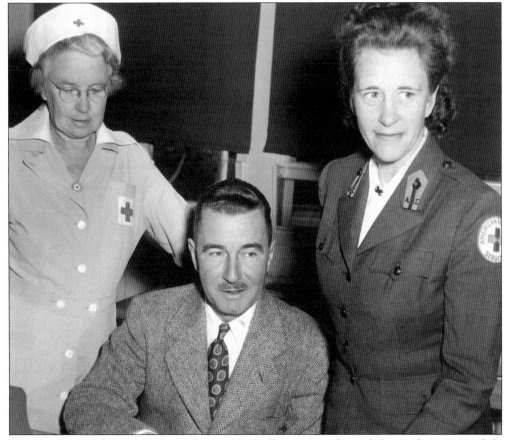

Veterans Hospital manager Gen. Francis W. Rollins pauses for a photograph in 1946 while conferring with Mrs. S.E. Smith (left), a Gray Lady, and Adelaide Kintz, a Red Cross field director. In the immediate aftermath of World War II, the Veterans Hospital was critical to the care and rehabilitation of US servicemen. The hospital requested Gray Lady volunteers to assist nurses, administrators, and patients.

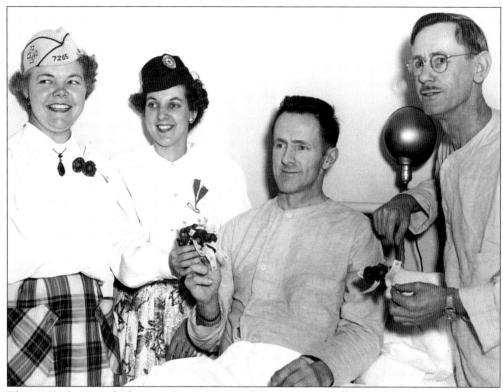

This 1952 photograph shows a "Poppy Days" celebration, originally created to honor those who died in World War I. After World War II, Poppy Days were adopted for fundraising by veterans hospitals. Disabled vets would make "Poppy Tags" as a symbol of their sacrifice. From left to right are Marie Rumberger, chairman, Livermore VFW Women's Auxiliary; Mrs. James Dolan, chairman, Livermore American Legion Women's Auxiliary; and Leonard Matson and Norman Benson, both recovering at Veterans Hospital.

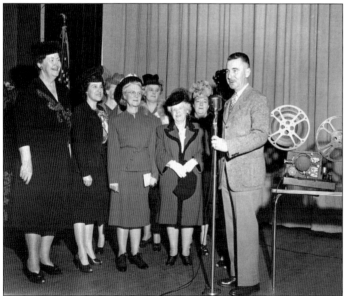

VA Hospital manager Gen. Francis W. Rollins thanks the California Federation of Women's Clubs for a donated 16-millimeter sound projector and screen in 1947. From left to right (first row) are Mrs. Benjamin F. Warner, president of the 78,000-member organization, Mrs. Marvin Herman, Mrs. Augustus Dunaway, Agnes E. Aller, and Mrs. Emmett Copeland; (second row) Mrs. H. Jewel Coun, Mrs. Henry LeRoy, and Mrs. Louis Le Fevre.

Six

Airports, Naval
Air Station, and
Laboratories

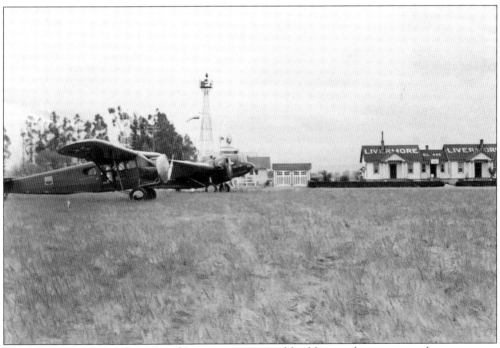

This 1935 view shows the original Livermore terminal building and government beacon tower. Richfield Oil Company built another beacon atop a 126-foot tower in 1928. It was one of 36 air guidance beacons from Mexico to Canada and could be seen along Highway 50 at night. The Livermore Intermediate Airport was designated a "Civil Emergency Airfield" in 1929 by the Civil Aeronautics Administration. The tower was removed in 1943 for safety during naval pilot training.

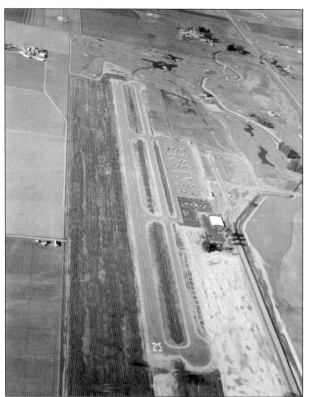

Livermore Municipal Airport is pictured between 1966 and 1969. In 1965, about 65 aircraft called the new airport home; that number grew to over 400 just 18 years later. This photograph was taken prior to construction of the terminal building, completed in 1969. In the upper right is the newly opened Las Positas Golf Course.

Hangers and aircraft are pictured at the original airport location after World War II. Livermore's airport began as a private dirt runway in 1929, west of Rincon Avenue and south of Portola Avenue. During World War II, the Navy took control and used it for training and as a secondary facility to the primary naval air station located off East Avenue. The airport was returned to civilian aviators in 1947 and renamed Sky Ranch.

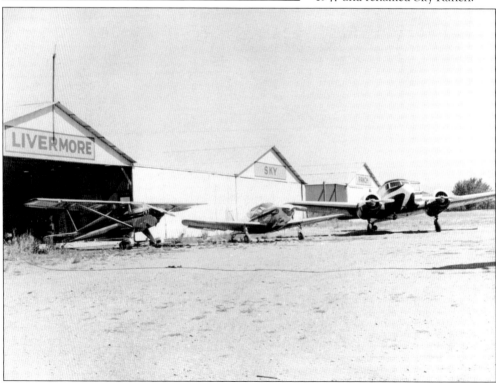

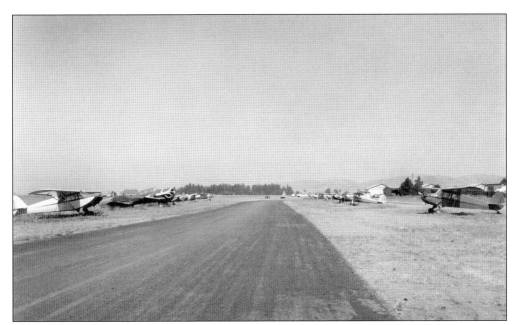

The dirt runway is visible in this photograph with aircraft parked along the side at Sky Ranch. A hanger is partially visible in the background. The US Navy paved the runway when it acquired the airport March 1942.

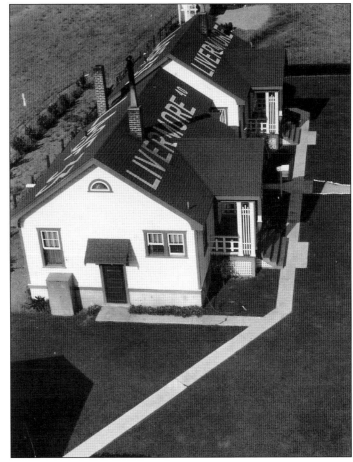

This c. 1935 aerial photograph shows the airport terminal with the building's "LASF 33" identification number visible.

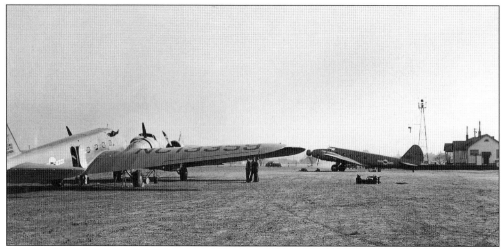

Some early, multiengine aircraft are visible in this c. 1935 photograph. In October 1940, a plane carrying Eleanor Roosevelt landed here, en route from Seattle to Los Angeles, when Oakland Airport was fogged in. John G. Roots, secretary of the Livermore Chamber of Commerce, welcomed Mrs. Roosevelt and presented her with a bottle of Livermore Valley wine. Close to 250 people came to the airport to see the first lady, who graciously posed for photographs and gave autographs.

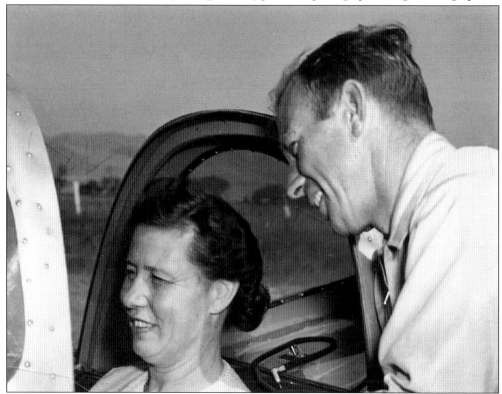

Flying out of the Livermore airport was not exclusive to men. Marfreda Coffin, a health nurse for the Livermore elementary and high schools, took flight lessons. This 1947 photograph shows Coffin at the controls of a single-seat aircraft conferring with William George. The Sky Ranch also provided crop dusting services to area farmers..

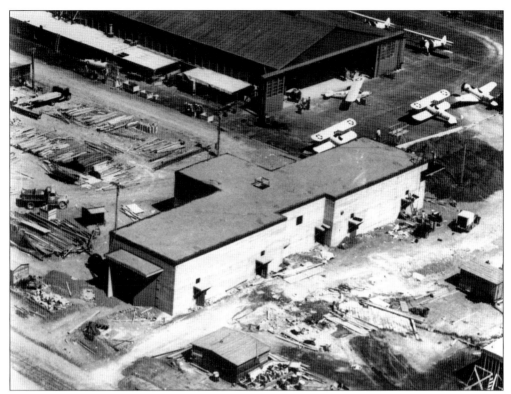

The US government bought 629 acres of Gatzmer Wagoner's ranch for $75,265 and built the Livermore Naval Air Station (NAS). This 1940 photograph of the eastern end of the station shows the mixture of aircraft used for training purposes. It eventually had its own fire department, photograph lab, security department, infirmary, commissary, and radio department.

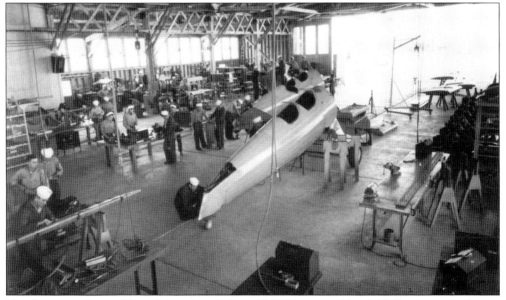

Naval personnel assemble training aircraft about 1942. Livermore Naval Air Station trained more than 4,000 air cadets during the war.

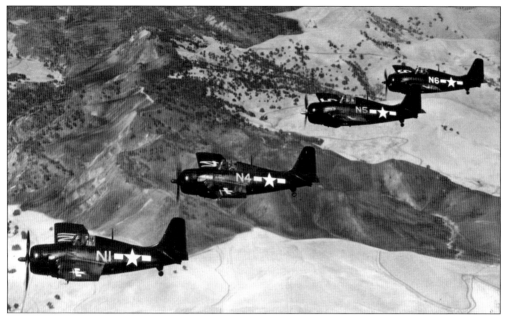

Four Grumman Wildcats fly in formation over the hills surrounding Livermore about 1943.

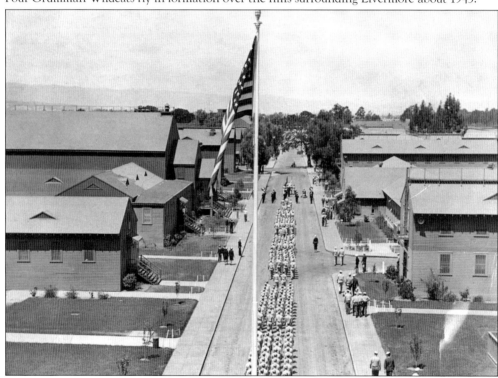

Navy personnel are on parade march on the South Mall through the naval air station. The station commanding officer was Capt. C.C. Champion Jr. These buildings would become the earliest facilities for the University of California Radiation Laboratory (UCRL) in 1952. The building in the left foreground housed the medical department. The building across the street became the magnetic fusion energy program building.

Naval aviation celebrates its birthday in 1945. The barracks in the background are for the Women Accepted for Volunteer Emergency Service (WAVES) and were on land now part of Sandia Laboratory. As the war came to an end that year, the naval station began to wind down its operations.

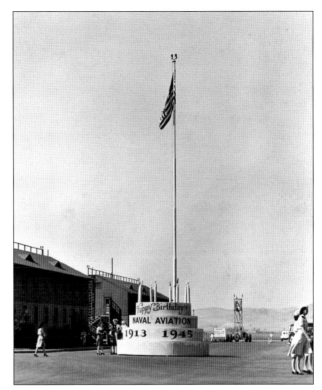

Navy personnel are on the march in 1943. The administrative building looms in the background. All station orders originated from this building. UCRL later used the structure as its administration building. Director Herbert F. York converted the infirmary's X-ray room, which had lead-lined walls, into a room for "classified discussion." This building would also house the first UCRL Univac I computer.

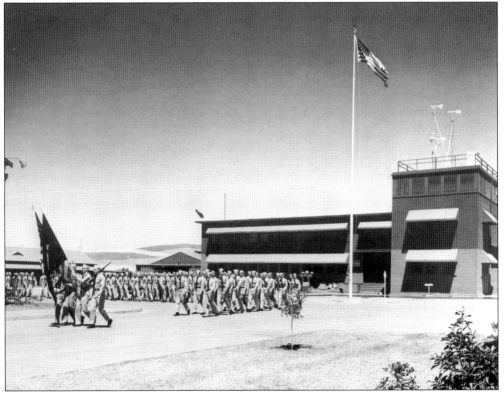

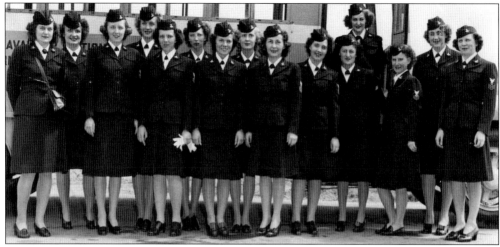

WAVES appear in the *Golden Gater*, the newsletter of the Livermore Naval Air Station. The photograph accompanies an article that describes their transfers to other bases. From left to right are M.I. Hagen, E.M. McKee, H.M. Holdsworth, D.D. Casebeer, G.A. Krzynowek, J.I. Rodgers, C.A. Niep, S.D. Wilson, M.L. Dempsey, A.H. Steinke, E.A. Guidone, H.M. Lewis, J.C. Pakiz, I.W. Hailes, and L.A. O'Rourke.

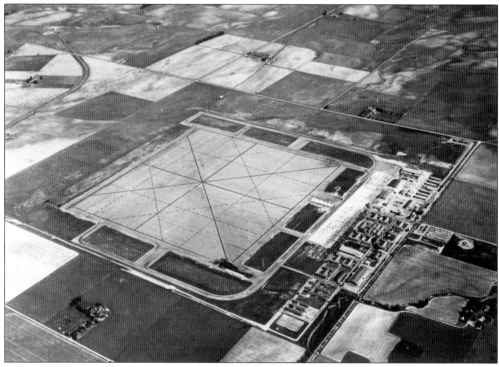

The Livermore Naval Air Station, pictured in 1944, shows crisscross patterns for practicing takeoff and landing positions. The base transitioned from pilot training to deployment staging for carrier air groups. Planes such as F6F Hellcat, F7F Tigercat, F4U Corsair fighters, TBM Avenger torpedo bombers, and SB2C Helldiver dive-bombers used the site for emergency landings and for overflow staging. After World War II, Livermore NAS was a naval reserve aircraft base until 1950, then transferred to the Atomic Energy Commission.

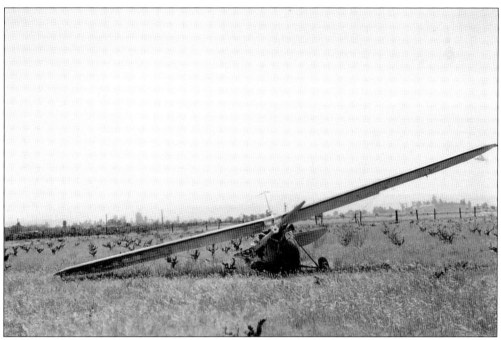

Not all landings were smooth at the airport. This photograph shows the aftermath of a hard landing in 1937. Too damaged to fly out, this plane had to wait in a vineyard for rescue.

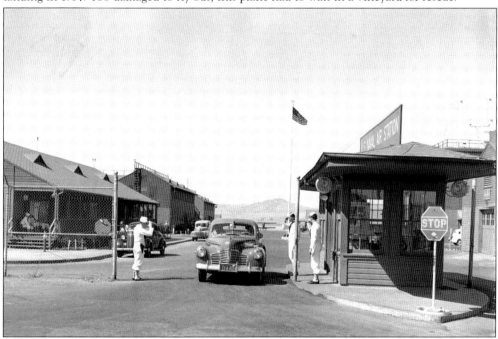

This parting view shows the naval air station entrance a few years before it became the nucleus of the University of California Radiation Laboratory (UCRL). The lab's first director, Herbert F. York, turned the naval training facility into a world-class laboratory. The name was changed to the Lawrence Radiation Laboratory in 1958 in tribute to one of the lab's architects, Ernest O. Lawrence, who died that year.

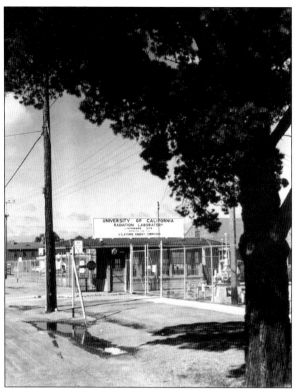

The entrance to the University of California Radiation Laboratory (UCRL), founded in 1952 by nuclear scientists Edward Teller and Ernest Lawrence, is pictured here. UCRL ("the Rad Lab") was an outgrowth of World War II. Scientists replaced soldiers on the Cold War front line against onetime ally the Soviet Union, developing weapons and tackling the engineering challenges facing a rapidly changing United States.

The East Avenue entrance to the laboratory with a sign directing visitors to California Research and Development (part of Standard Oil) is pictured here. The lab began with only 72 employees. In 1954, a 90-inch cyclotron was installed and remained until 1971. Housing developments had not yet stretched this far on East Avenue. By the 1960s, Sandia and the lab employed over 450 PhDs.

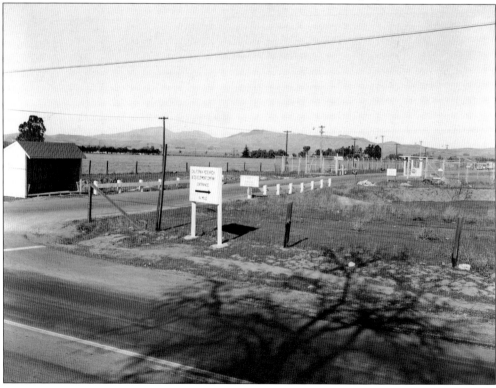

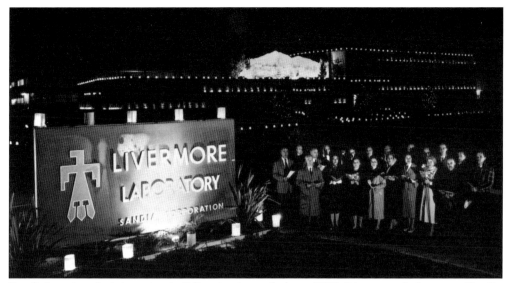

Sandia's main administration building is pictured about 1960. Livermore Laboratory Sandia Corporation began operation in March 1956 and had over 1,000 employees by 1965. Located across the street from UCRL, Sandia provided engineering support to designing delivery systems and mechanisms for nuclear weapons. During the Cold War, Sandia Lab also tracked nuclear weapons. Sandia Livermore is one of three Sandia facilities; Sandia New Mexico and Sandia Tonopoh Nevada are the others.

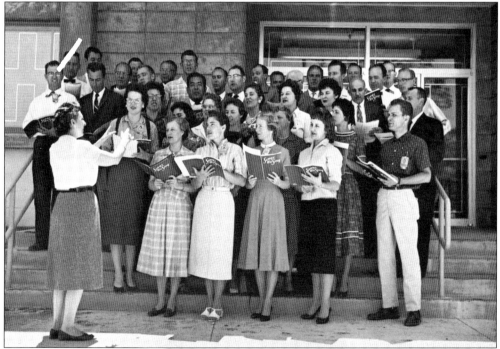

The Sandia choir, the Classified Chords, is pictured about 1960. Lab employees brought their interest for art and culture to Livermore. They were also at the forefront in promoting slow and responsible growth for the city. The *Independent*, a local newspaper, and SAVE were heavily influenced by the laboratory employees and helped the community project a common voice.

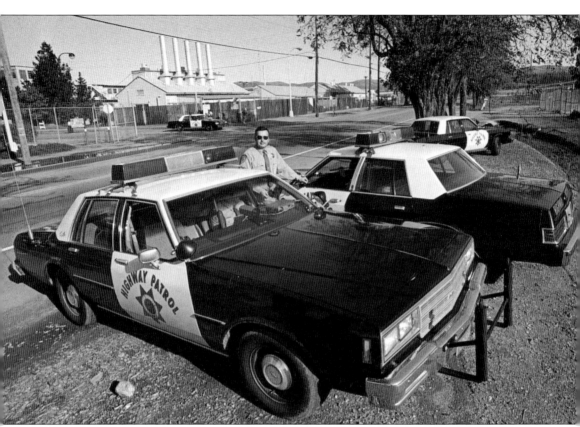

California Highway patrolman Kendall McAllister awaits a planned protest in 1982 at the main entrance to the lab. As one of the nation's two nuclear weapons laboratories, Livermore remained a focus for protests, especially on May Day and Good Friday. On this occasion, 60 people were expected for a noontime rally. A larger protest at Sproul Plaza in Berkeley usurped the local event, and no one showed up here.

Seven

SCHOOLS, STUDENTS, AND FACULTY

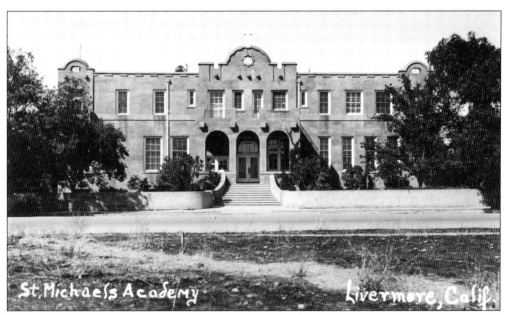

This c. 1935 E.J. Lawless photograph shows St. Michael's Academy at the northeast corner of Fourth and Maple Streets. Built in September 1913, it opened with 30 students. By late 1940, enrollment was 216; 10 years later, it climbed to 400 students. Two classrooms were added to the original school in 1960. In 2004, this facility was razed and a new facility was constructed and dedicated by Allen H. Vigneron, Catholic Bishop of Oakland.

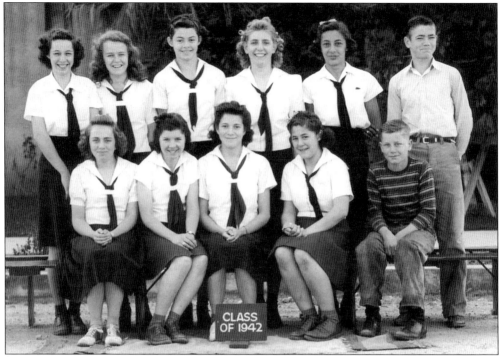

The St. Michael's Class of 1942 is pictured here. From left to right are (front row) Jean Koudelka, Dorothy Stanley, Doris Magee, Rose Palldino, and Walter Jensen; (back row) Frances O'Neil, Elizabeth Beaudet, Shirley Nevin, Elizabeth Croce, Madeline Genoni, and Joseph Regan. Not pictured is Joseph Leal. Graduates were treated to a breakfast hosted by St. Michael's Mother's Club, at which they presented the class will, announced the valedictorian, and invited graduating students to speak to younger students.

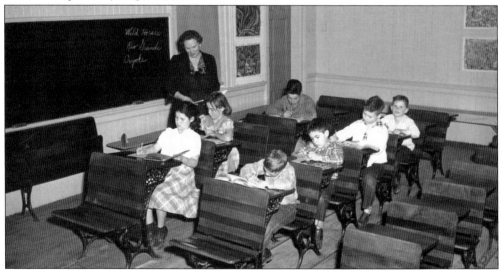

Rural migration to the suburbs trumped the baby boom, and enrollment at rural schools, such as Summit (shown 1951), declined in the 1950s. Summit closed three years later due to lack of students. Irene Nickerson Armstrong graduated from Summit in 1911 and taught there from 1943 to 1954. In 1968, Inman School, another rural school, closed after 100 years of operation.

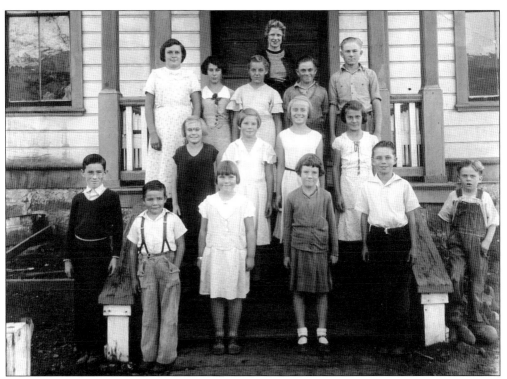

The 1933 Summit School class photograph shows the range of ages attending the one-room schoolhouse. Pictured, from left to right, are (first row) Jean Egan, Billy Arsenarlt, Eleanor Croak, Alice Allen, Billy Armstrong, and Lester Fachner; (second row) Stella Fachner, Georgiana Allen, Verna Fachner, and Margaret Mohr; (third row) Evelyn Mohr, Gertrude Egan, Rae Madsen, Ruddy Fachner, and Dan Fachner; (fourth row) teacher Leona Lassen.

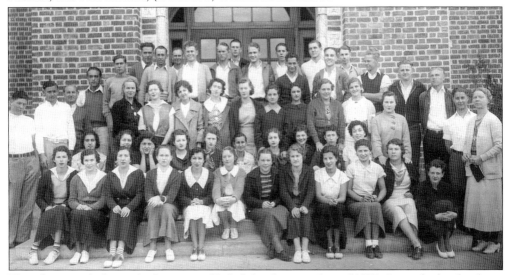

This photograph shows the Livermore High School senior class of 1935. A new high school was built at East Avenue and Maple Street for $137,755 and dedicated in May 1930. The previous high school was located on Eighth Street between H and G Streets. In 1937, the brick facade was covered in concrete as part of a WPA project. Enrollment in 1942 was 300 students.

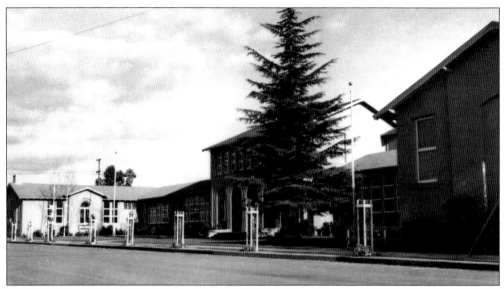

Fifth Street School, pictured about 1935, was designed in 1922 by local architect Henry M Myers, who had been a student at the old Livermore Grammar School on the same site (block bounded by Fifth, J, Seventh, and I Streets). The Fifth Street School enrolled 500 students in 1930. In the same year, Livermore High School graduated 55 students.

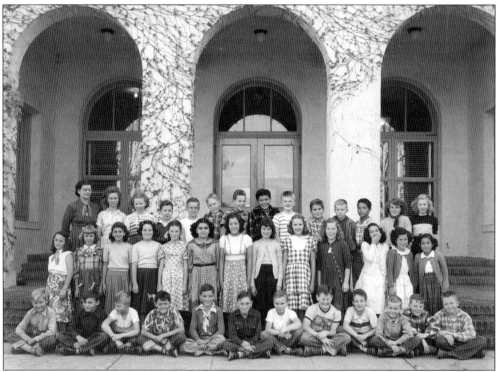

This is the 1951–1952 class portrait of the Fifth Street School. The boy making the funny face in the front row is Edward Cassidy. In 1944, Fifth Street employed 17 staff, including a custodian who also drove the school bus. In 1950, Fifth Street was Livermore's sole elementary school; in 1969, it had an average daily attendance of 586 students.

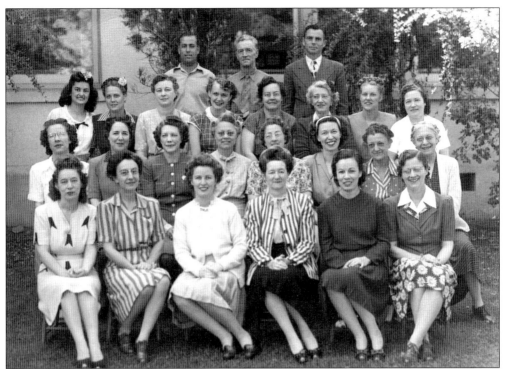

Fifth Street School faculty members are pictured above in 1947 and below in 1953. The increase in staff and teachers reflects the rate of Livermore's post–World War II population growth. By 1969, Livermore's schools had 16 principals, 5 vice principals, 356 teachers, and 4 librarians. The Livermore Valley Unified School District then had a budget of $9,701,500. The annual growth rate was about 800 students per year between 1961 through 1969.

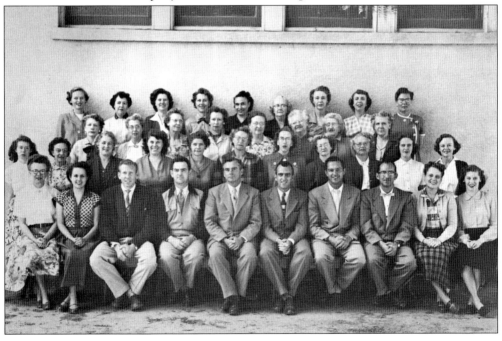

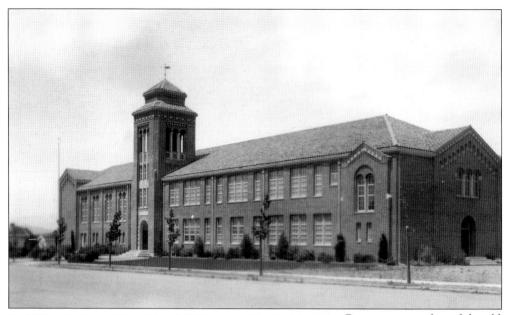

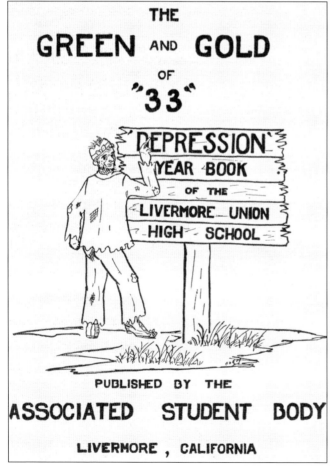

THE
GREEN AND GOLD
OF
"33"

"DEPRESSION"
YEAR BOOK
OF THE
LIVERMORE UNION
HIGH SCHOOL

PUBLISHED BY THE
ASSOCIATED STUDENT BODY
LIVERMORE, CALIFORNIA

Concern over safety of the old Union High School resulted in construction of a modern Livermore High School building, dedicated on March 4, 1930. In 1937, the Works Progress Administration (WPA) covered the brickwork in concrete as reinforcement against earthquake damage. By the 1950s, the campus included a science building, a library, a shop, two additional classroom buildings, two gyms, and a student union.

Highlighting concern over the national depression, the Livermore High School yearbook team created a theme for the 1933 *Green and Gold*. Each class was given a nickname to tell the story of those difficult years. Seniors were "Vagabonds," juniors "Tramps," sophomores "Hoboes," and freshmen "Baby Bums."

This photograph shows Livermore High School yearbook art for the sophomore "Hoboes." In 1933, the Livermore High School graduating "Vagabonds" would "solemnly swear that the only way to get through high school is to bum. We found through four long years of experience that we like to bum, the teachers liked us to bum, and so bum we did."

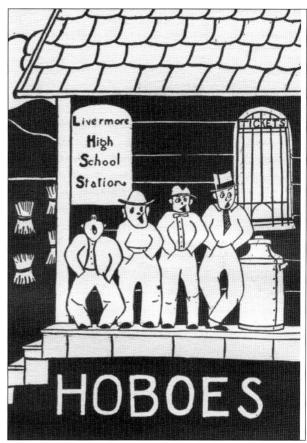

The Livermore High School 1952 yearbook informal senior portraits are pictured here. Students of Livermore High reflect an increasing draw to the automobile: "A favorite place in which seniors are found / is the automobile, if there is one around. / Here in spite of the crowd, there is just room enough, / but instead of John Reholder's, the Smitty's Rolls-Ruff."

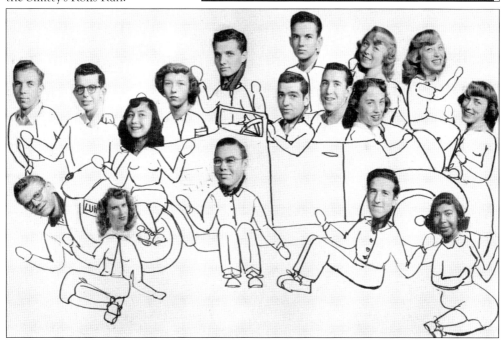

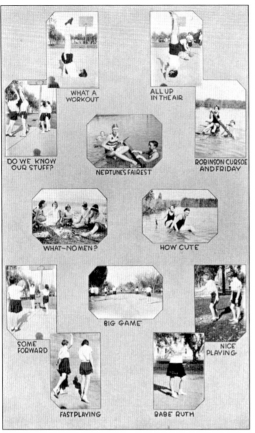

The Livermore High School 1930 yearbook informal portraits are pictured here. The 40 members of the graduating class of 1930 were the first in the new Livermore High School building, replacing Union High School No. 1.

The Livermore High School Marching Cowboys Band is pictured here in 1952.

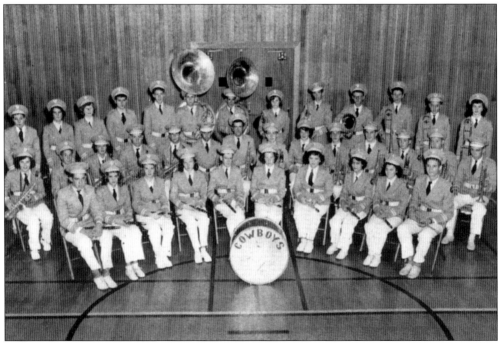

The main entrance to Livermore High School in 1932 is pictured at the right, two years after its construction. In 1937, a WPA project changed the exterior look of the school. The image below depicts the Livermore High School Cadet Company around 1945, performing a ceremony honoring a former student killed in action during World War II. The cadet company was established in 1943. During World War II, 12 Livermore High alumni were killed in action.

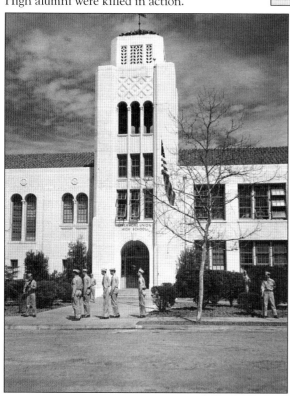

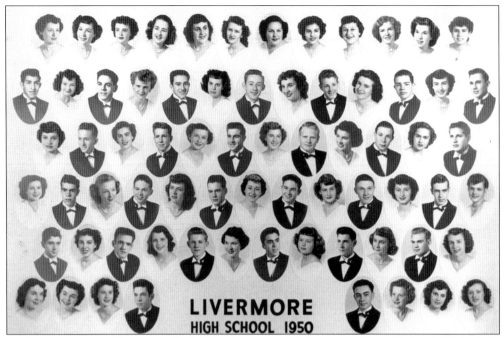

LIVERMORE
HIGH SCHOOL 1950

Graduating seniors of Livermore High School are pictured above in 1950 and below 1957. In 1950, as suburban development began in earnest, there were more than 4,000 residents in Livermore and 72 graduates of LHS. By 1957, there were almost 13,000 residents and 109 graduates. In 1965, Livermore's High School and the three grammar schools formed the Valley Joint Unified School District.

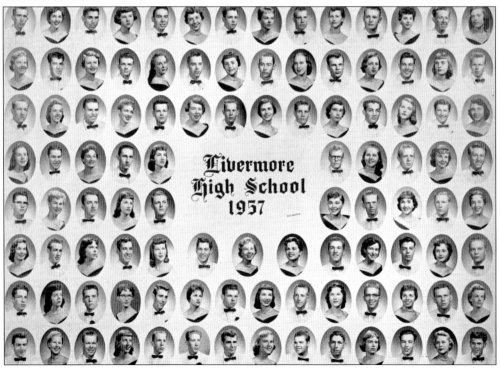

Livermore
High School
1957

Here, a construction crew sets the post for lighting the Livermore High School field in 1947, which allowed fans to enjoy the Cowboys on Friday nights.

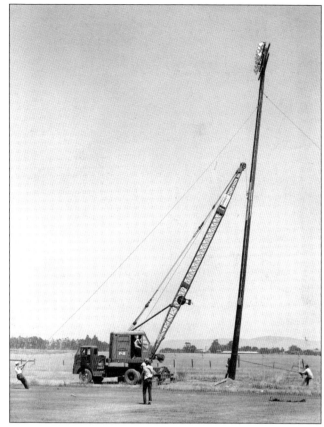

The Livermore High School Board of Trustees is pictured here in 1948. From left to right are Thornton K. Taylor, Maitland R. Henry, Sam F. Ray, school board president William J. Bonetti, and Dr. Donald M. Fraser.

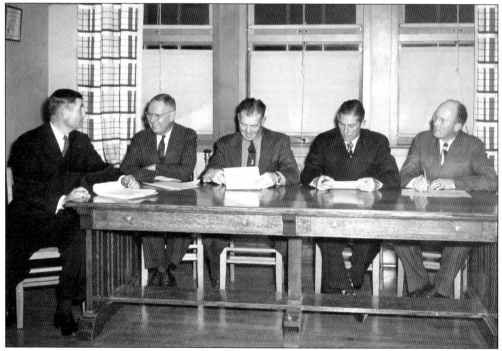

93

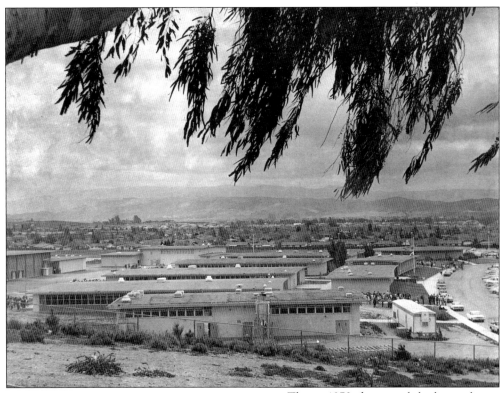

This c. 1970 photograph looks south from Oak Knoll Cemetery at Granada High School. The growth of elementary school enrollments in the 1950s foreshadowed the need to open another high school. Granada opened in 1964, with the black-and-gold Matadors mascot. The Livermore High Cowboys are the chief rival of the Matadors. Mascots of both schools reflect the rural roots of an expanding Livermore.

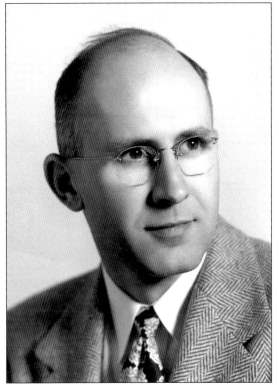

Livermore High School principal E.E. Rundstorm came to Livermore in 1946 and served the school district for more than 31 years. Beginning his career at Livermore High as a math and science teacher, he was active in the planning and construction of numerous schools, including Granada High School. Rundstorm served as the Livermore Valley Joint Unified School District's superintendent from 1969 to 1973.

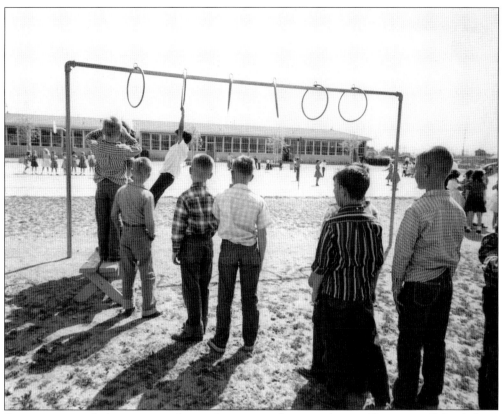

Boys wait patiently for a turn on the monkey rings at Junction Avenue Elementary School about 1960. Attire includes no T-shirts or shorts, girls all in skirts, and boys in button-down shirts.

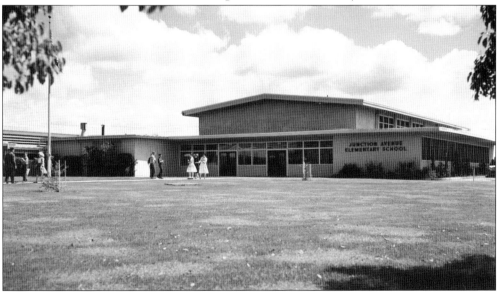

Junction Avenue Elementary School, pictured about 1960, opened in 1951 to accommodate the influx of children in the post–World War II baby boom. Junction and Fifth Street School were the elementary schools in town.

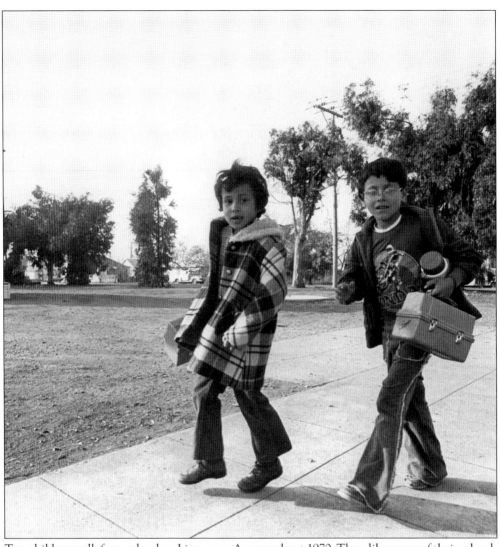

Two children walk from school on Livermore Avenue about 1970. They, like many of their school-age peers, were part of a new generation of kids born and raised in Livermore.

Eight

SPORTS

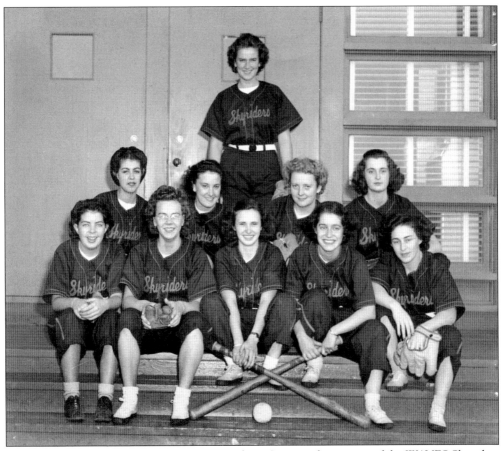

In addition to their service at Livermore Naval Air Station, the women of the WAVES Skyriders softball team found time for recreation and fun around 1945.

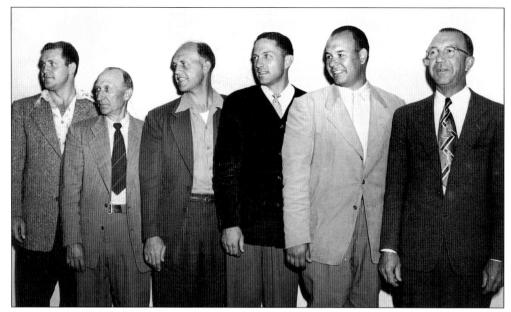

Livermore High School's 1951 winning coaches are, from left to right, Irving Trafin (assistant coach, football and basketball); K.O. "Spike" Hunter (baseball); "Herm" Mettler (head coach, football and track); Tony Winn (basketball); and Ben Snyder (swimming). At far right is principal Ralph T. Wattenburger. 1951 was a banner year for LHS sports, with the football and basketball teams both winning East Bay Counties Athletic League championships.

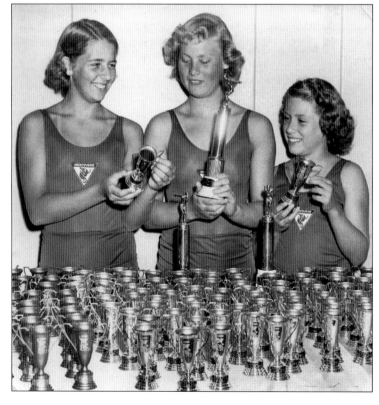

AquaCowboys, from left to right, Carolyn Wattenburger, Nancy Farnam, and Judy Meyers pose with trophies from the 1951 awards ceremony from Livermore Area Recreation and Parks District's (LARPD) annual Junior Summer Olympics. The group was formed in 1950 with the purpose of "competitive aquatics." By 1968, the team had 80 swimmers participating in regional and national competitions with a few AquaCowboys participating in the Olympic trials in Los Angeles.

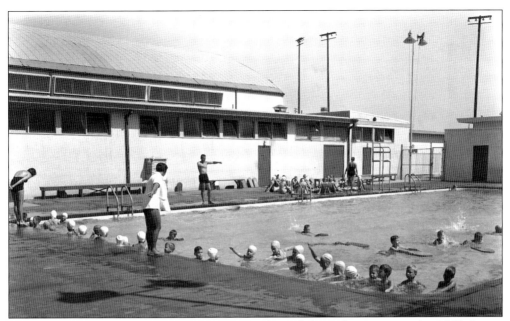

Livermore High School's pool opened in 1948 and was dedicated as a memorial to LHS alumni World War II veterans. A *Memory Book of Our Gold Stars* describing the circumstances of each soldier's fate was written by the English IV class of 1946. Those alumni include Peter J. Barthe, Robert G. Holm, Thomas V. Kelly Jr., Nathan B. MacLean, Franklyn W. Mueller, Howard V. Munton, Arnold W. Paul, L. William Reifschneider, Ormond B. Smith, Edward F. Teeter, John R. Thornton, and former science teacher Coyle Hillard. A plaque honoring them was installed near the judge's shack and is still there today. In the 1950s, the pool played host to the AquaCowboys, an independent swim club that used the pool for practice and swim meets. The AquaRodeo of 1953 was billed as being the largest swim meet in the nation that year.

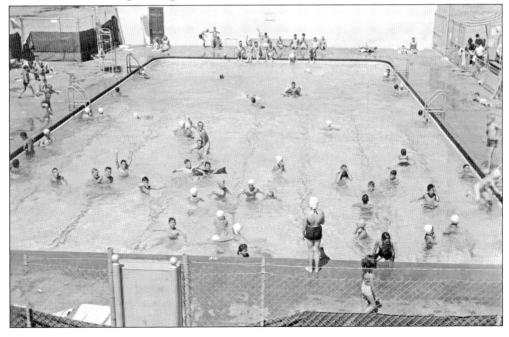

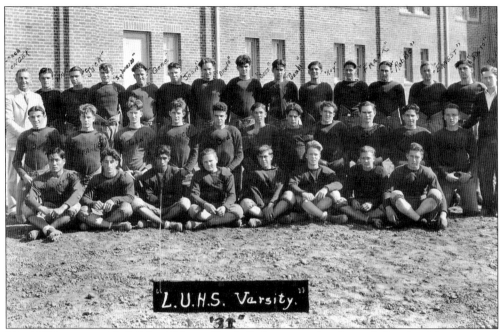

The 1931 Livermore High School Varsity Football players stand with coach Stanley Gibson next to a portion of the newly opened Livermore High School. In a nine-game season, the team won four, lost four, and tied one (6-6 against Pleasanton). The team tied for second place in its division.

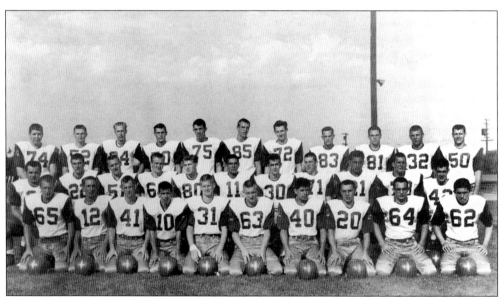

The 1959 Livermore High School team captured a perfect season, going 9-0. Pictured are, from left to right, (top row) R. Martinez, L. Anderson, L. Strieff, C. Frank, B. Ranney, T. Daily, B. Balanda, B. Housh, P. Kiss, S. Gimbel, and R. Schrader; (middle row) L. Howard, R. Mueller, J. Hughes, B. Palmer, D. Dunaway, R. Rochin, R. Buckley, D. Hansen, J. Aflague, P. Phillips, and B. Clark; (bottom row) J. Needham, D. Strieff, J. Ingledue, W. Walker, D. Dunham, C. Neill, R. Garcia, T. Favero, P. Hurley, and D. Schuchardt.

The 1933 Livermore High School "B" basketball team is pictured here. These young men clearly benefitted from the new high school sports facilities, built only three years earlier. They won the Southern Alameda County Athletic League Championship. From left to right are Ellsworth Cragholm, Bobby Haera, Joe Felix, Bobby Santos, and Johnny Roderick.

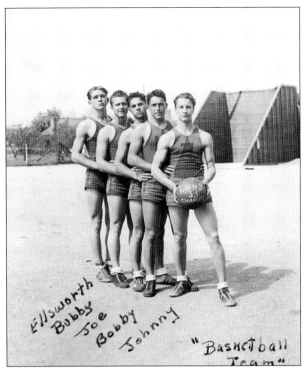

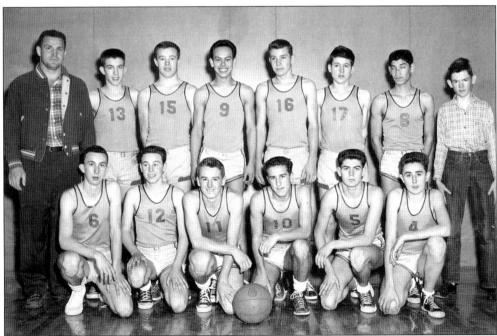

The 1950 Livermore High School's "B" basketball team photo includes, from left to right, (first row) B. Huddleston, W. Escover, G. Kelly, R. Rego, J. Sarboraria, and J. Rex; (second row) coach Irving Trafin, R. Hoffman, T. Rehder, R. McGlinchey, D. Ralph, W. Way, P. Coronando, and manager D. Smith. The team lost five of its first seven games but eventually won 11 straight victories to win a co-championship.

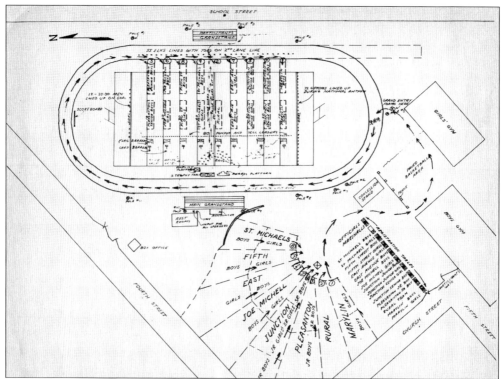

A 1961 Twin Valley Relay Parade map is shown above. Below, teams are pictured on the Livermore High School field at the opening ceremonies of the event. Al Caffodio, owner of the Village Canteen (1951–1968), organized the first relay in 1958 as a giant track meet with 394 young competitors and a theme of "Everybody Wins." Everyone received a trophy for participating. In 1962, the event expanded to 1,368 participants. The relay was held at the LHS track with proceeds benefiting the Livermore Elementary School Band Fund. LARPD named a park (located off Shawnee Road) after Al Caffodio in 1968 when he died.

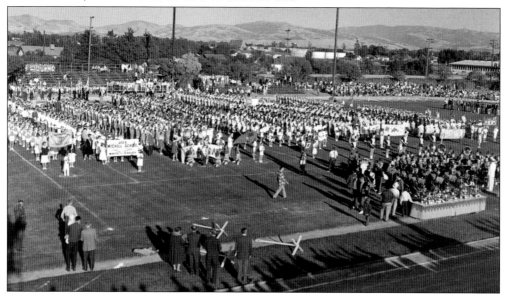

Norris Dutcher poses with his *Dutch Treat* speedboat, which won two events at the 1946 National Speedboat Championship at Long Beach, California, in "Racing" and "Service Runabout." The image appears in *Sea* magazine.

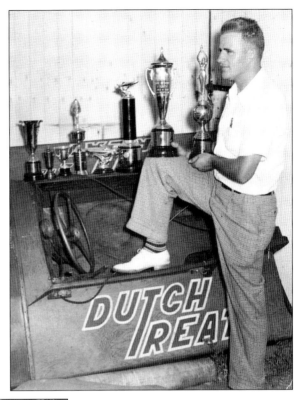

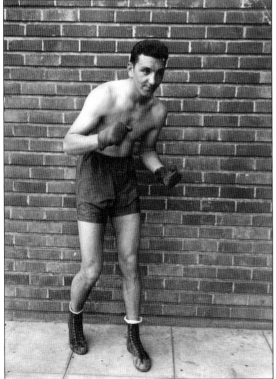

Bill Radunich (San Jose, pictured) fought Charlie Thomas (Oakland) for the title of 1938 Amateur Heavyweight in an event hosted by the Livermore American Legion. Radunich knocked out Thomas in the first round with two minutes on the clock. The two had previously squared off in another Livermore Legion–sponsored fight, prompting the *Livermore Herald* to quip: "History DOES repeat itself. Lightning DOES strike twice in the same place."

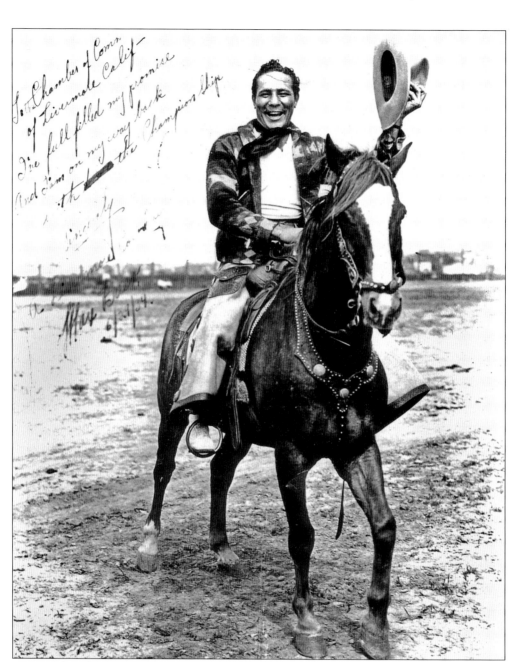

Here, a playful Max Baer (1934) poses triumphantly on horseback in full cowboy regalia. A handwritten note from the boxing champ reads: "To the Chamber of Commerce of Livermore Calif—I've fulfilled my promise and I am on my way back with the Championship. Sincerely, A Livermore Cowboy, Max Baer, 6/29/34." He won the 1934 Heavyweight Championship at the peak of the Depression and had a hall of fame record of 72 wins (53 by knockouts) and 12 losses. The *Livermore Herald* devoted a weekly column called Baer Facts to follow his success. He continued to make public appearances throughout Livermore until his death in 1959.

Nine

Wine and Agriculture

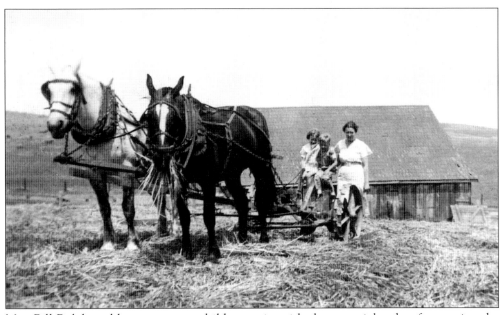

Mrs. Bill Ralph and her two young children assist with the essential tasks of managing the Ralph's ranch about 1935. Livermore's vineyards, ranches, and farms were an important part of the city's history during the Depression and in postwar growth. Many of Livermore's ranches remain family-run operations today.

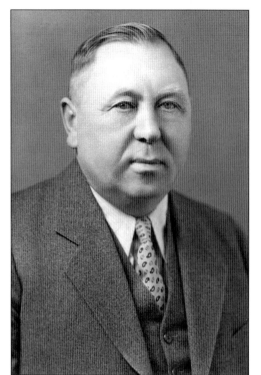 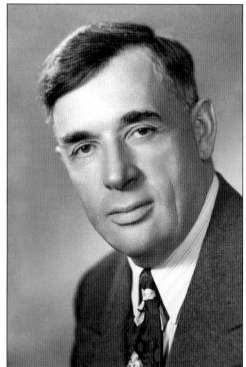

Founder Carl Wente began producing wine in 1883. His sons, Ernest and Herman, ran the business through the Depression, World War II, into the 1970s. Ernest Wente, pictured on the left (around 1955) was born July 9, 1890, and was the second student to enroll at the University of California, Davis. He participated in the University of California Berkeley's Regional Oral History Project in 1969. Those interviews are still accessible through the Regional Oral History Office (ROHO) and the Livermore Heritage Guild. He died October 21, 1980, having worked in Livermore's wine industry his entire career. Herman L. Wente, as vice president and general manager of Wente Winery, is pictured on the right (around 1955). He managed the business side, while Ernest was out in the field experimenting with different varieties of vines and soil. Herman died in 1961.

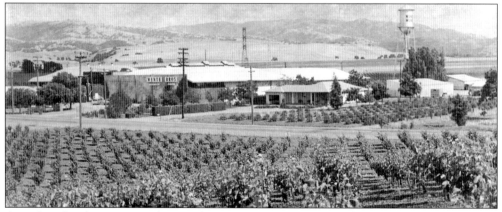

A modern bottling process plant at the Wente Winery is pictured in 1969. At that time, the winery owned 800 acres and produced over 25,000 cases. Prior to Prohibition, the winery only produced bulk wine. The Wente label appeared after Prohibition in 1934, specializing in white varietals such as pinot blanc, chardonnay, sauvignon blanc, and white burgundy.

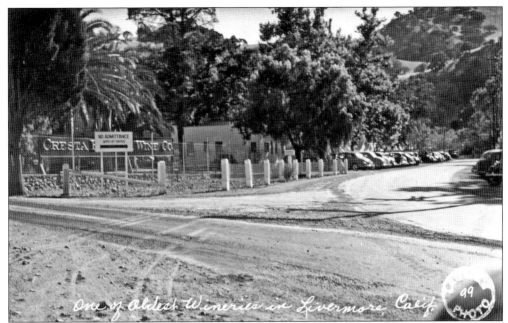

One of Oldest Wineries in Livermore Calif

Cresta Blanca Winery, located at the present site of Wente Sparkling Cellars, was established in 1882 by Charles A. Wetmore. Cresta Blanca, pictured about 1940, remained operational through Prohibition and was sold to Schenley Distillers in 1942. It promoted the label to a larger audience through magazine advertisements and radio programs and sponsored a radio program called *The Cresta Blanca Carnival* (1942–1944), which was hosted by Jack Pearl and conductor Morton Gould and featured different musical genres. This was followed by *Cresta Blanca's Hollywood Players* on CBS Tuesday nights in 1946, which featured Hollywood stars like Bette Davis, Claudette Colbert, Joan Fontaine, Gene Kelly, and Gregory Peck. Ian Fleming's novel *Diamonds are Forever* features James Bond's signature martini served with Cresta Blanca vermouth. A 1954 advertisement for the vermouth is shown below. Wente bought the property in 1961.

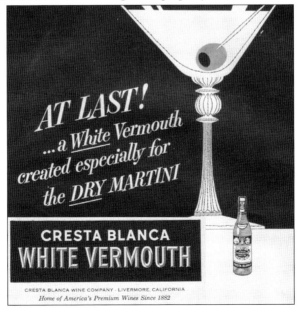

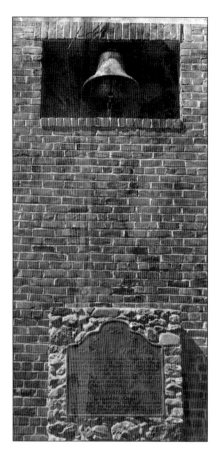

Founded in 1883, Concannon was one of a handful of wineries producing sacramental wine during Prohibition. The winery achieved State of California Historical Landmark (no. 641) status in 1958; the monument is pictured at left. In the photograph below, Joseph Concannon is flanked by flag-bearers at a flagpole dedication at the Concannon House on May 24, 1939. The flagpole was forged by a local blacksmith, and a local utility crew assembled and raised it. The plaque at the base of the flagpole honors two Army recruiters who had worked with Joseph, who himself was a captain in the US Army in 1918. In 1943, short of men to harvest the vineyard, the winery used personnel from the naval air station to pick grapes. Concannon wine went to the Vatican during World War II even though the United States was at war with Italy. Joseph Concannon received a medal from Pope John XXIII after the war.

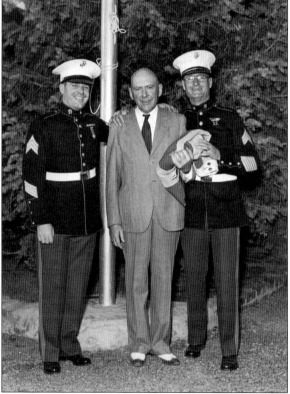

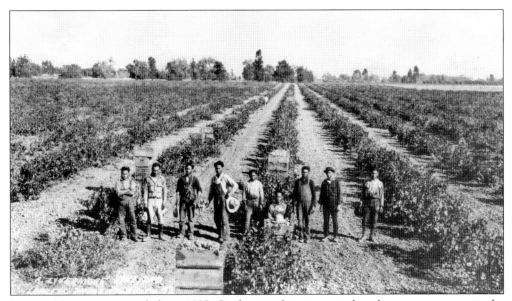

Grape pickers are pictured about 1935. Cool, westerly ocean winds reduce temperatures in the evenings, gravel-rich soil provides good drainage, and moderate winters combine to make the Livermore Valley optimal for growing wine grapes.

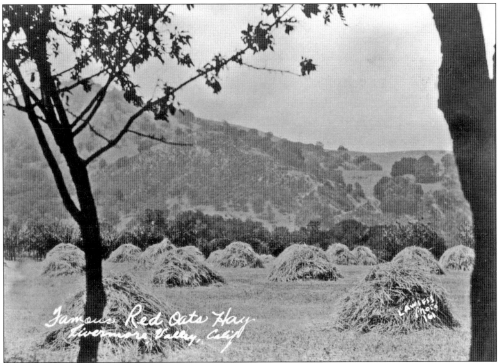

Famous as racehorse feed, red oats hay was a product of the dry farming method used by Livermore's grain growers. In the 1931 *Oakland Tribune Year Book*, the lead article on Livermore boasts of its "new construction, abundant harvest, and sustained prosperity." In the prior year, 158 railcar loads of wheat and barley along with 328 carloads of hay were shipped from the Livermore Depot. This is a c. 1935 E.J. Lawless photograph.

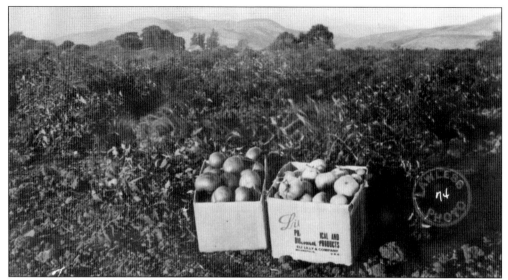

The commercial production of tomatoes in Livermore began with 800 acres in 1934. During World War II, the labor scarcity affected the agricultural harvest and even high school students helped pick tomatoes. With an estimated 35,000 tons of tomatoes on vines in 1942, the chamber of commerce requested stores be closed for two days so all available hands could help. Off-duty sailors from the naval air station assisted in the harvest at Gomes, Hagemann, Taylor, Pereira, and Wagoner farms. This is a c. 1935 Lawless Drug photograph.

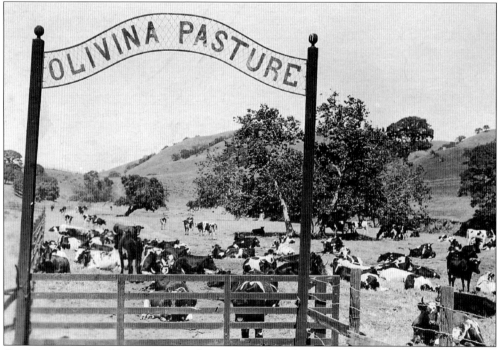

Cattle graze in the Olivina pasture about 1945. The Olivina Winery was established in 1881 by Julius P. Smith. Its name came from a combination of "*olive* and *vina* (wine)." Cattle helped wineries survive Prohibition until the repeal in 1933. Charles D. Crohare bought Olivina land in the 1940s, using it primarily as grazing land.

Two beautiful views show the Crosby Ranch (1963), nestled in the hills of the Arroyo Del Valle canyon south of Livermore. William Crosby, a Civil War veteran (Maine regiment), practiced law in San Francisco in 1882 and bought the property in 1887. The home was built in 1908 and named Mulfontes, from the Latin meaning "Many Springs." The home featured three fireplaces, a huge living room, and a wide porch below the ridge of the canyon. To the east of the Crosby Ranch, Cedar Mountain rises to 3,670 feet. A reunion in 1956 saw the gathering of four generations of Bernals, three of Crosbys, and Winegar and Sachau families at the ranch.

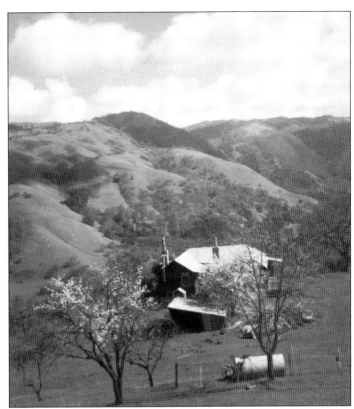

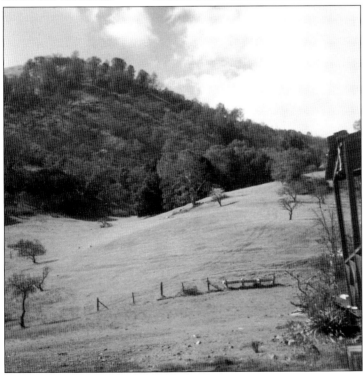

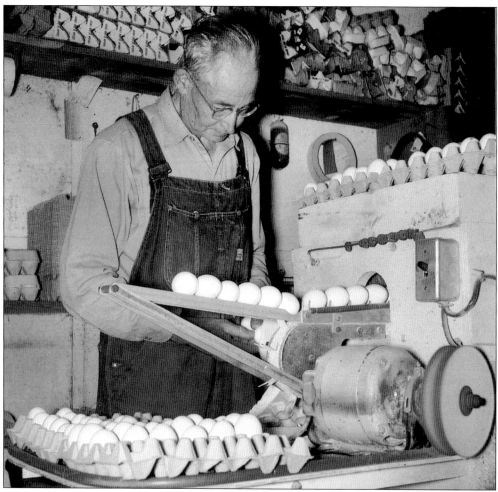

Graham Barber is pictured at the egg-washing machine around 1950. The Barber family raised chickens in Livermore beginning in 1911. In 1919, they purchased 24.59 acres at East and Hillcrest Avenues. J.H. Barber formed several organizations to advance the industry, including the Poultry Producers of Central California in 1917 and the California Poultry Improvement Association in 1935. The Verde Poultry Farm is pictured below around 1930. In 1937, the Livermore branch of the Poultry Producers of Central California reported that the community had between 500 and 600 commercial flocks producing 15,000 to 20,000 cases of eggs, generating approximately $100,000 in income to the poultrymen.

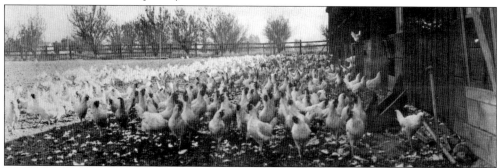

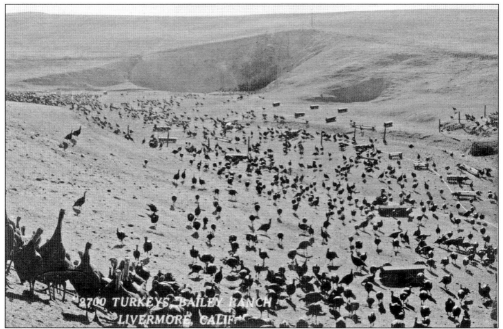

In addition to chickens, turkeys were also raised outside of town. This c. 1930 E.J. Lawless photograph shows 2,700 turkeys at Bailey Ranch. The Carlisle Ranch and the Mingoia's Turkey ranch are mentioned in articles or ads in the *Livermore Herald* and *Livermore News* in the 1930s and 1940s.

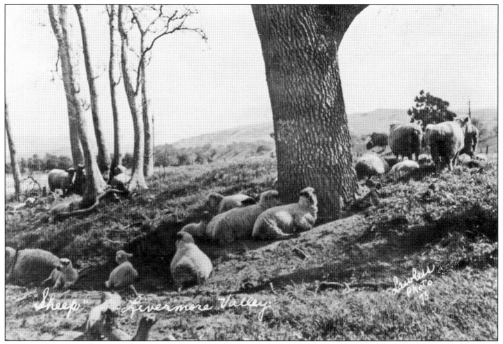

This Lawless Drug photograph shows Livermore sheep about 1930. Sheep were first introduced in the Livermore Valley by the Spanish in the late 1700s. Over 12,450 lambs and 265,000 pounds of wool were shipped out of town by train in 1930.

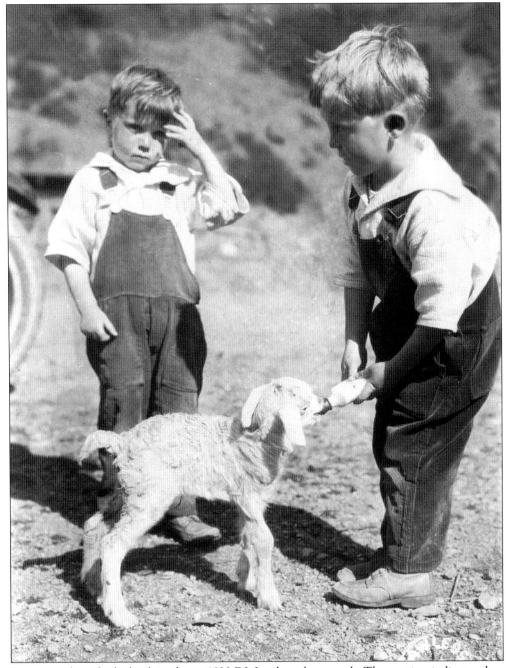

Two young boys feed a lamb in this c. 1930 E.J. Lawless photograph. The caption indicates they are descendents of William Mendenhall, founder of the town of Livermore.

Ten

PARADES AND EVENTS

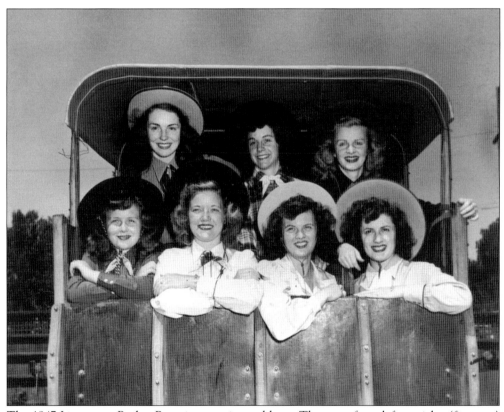

The 1947 Livermore Rodeo Beauties are pictured here. They are, from left to right, (first row) Barbara Hachman, Peggy Regan, Nancy Nickerson, and Noel Johnson; (second row) Joan Mitchell, Joy Mitchell, and Merilyn "Tilli" Holm. Livermore's first rodeo was held in 1918 to meet the city's $12,000 obligation to the Red Cross.

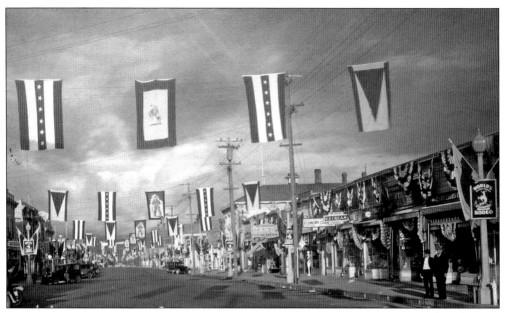

First Street is pictured in this 1932 image, looking west as downtown decorates for the rodeo. In the depths of the Great Depression, the residents of Livermore saw the rodeo as an indispensable tradition. Verda Holm was the Rodeo Queen in 1932. Three years later, "The World's Fastest Rodeo" was first used to describe the fast action of events and speed at which the next participant moved out of the chutes.

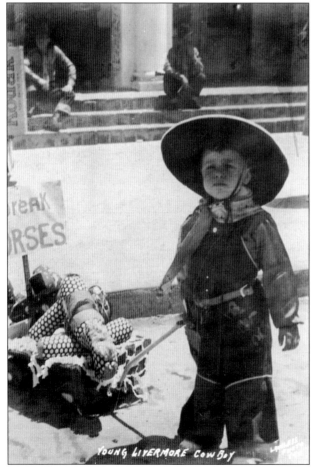

This young cowboy prepares to take his place in the Rodeo Parade in this c. 1930 E.J. Lawless photograph. Since 1918, the event has brought civic clubs, schoolchildren, local business, and cowboys together to celebrate the town's Hispanic heritage.

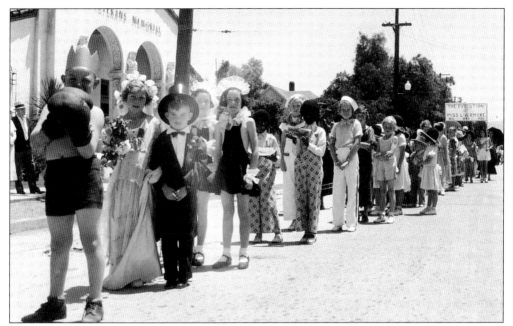

Louis Santucci—clad in trunks, crown, and gloves paying homage to his uncle and world champion boxer Max Baer—lines up for the Children's Rodeo Parade in front of the Veterans Memorial Building. The parade started promptly at 12:30 p.m. in June 1935, and a costume competition with cash prizes was open to all children of grammar school age. Louis won first prize ($2.50). An oral history by Louis's mother, Francis Santucci (Max Baer's sister), is available at the Livermore Heritage Guild.

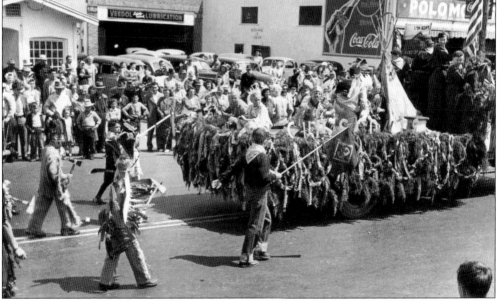

Boy Scouts of Livermore march in formation about 1950. During World War II, the Boy Scouts partnered with other civic groups and held regular scrap drives to collect much-needed materials to help sustain the war effort. They were recognized by the community every year with a spot in the parade for their continued good work in Livermore.

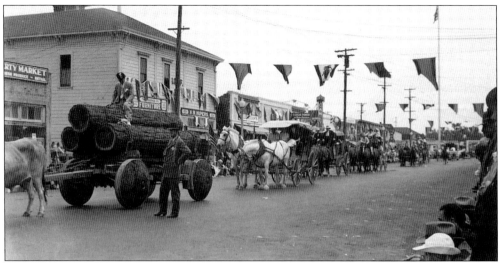

This timber wagon parades in front of the Odd Fellows Building in 1932. Hand-built by Martin Luther Marsh in 1848, it was used to haul lumber from the Sierra Nevada to Nevada City. In 1931, Martin's grandson Carl donated the wagon to the chamber of commerce, which used it to promote the rodeo and parade.

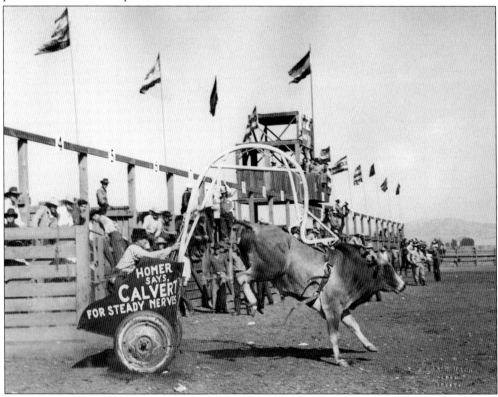

Homer Holcomb, a famous rodeo clown, demonstrates an easier way to handle a raging bull ride in 1944. Holcomb performed in the rodeo between 1930 and 1950. He saved Johnie Schneider in 1939 when a Brahman bull knocked him to the ground. In 1949, Holcomb signed a contract with Republic Studios and acted in Western movies.

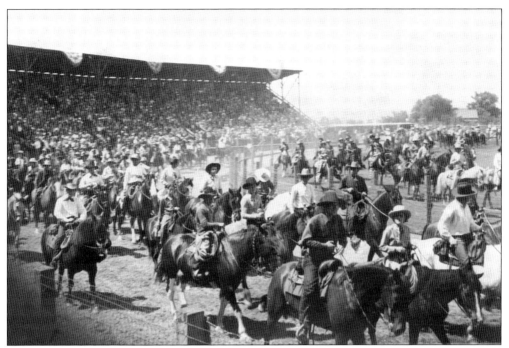

Each day of the rodeo, a horse parade commenced downtown on First Street, then traveled south on Livermore Avenue, and entered the rodeo grounds, where it would join the Grand Entry, as seen in this c. 1930 Lawless Drug photograph.

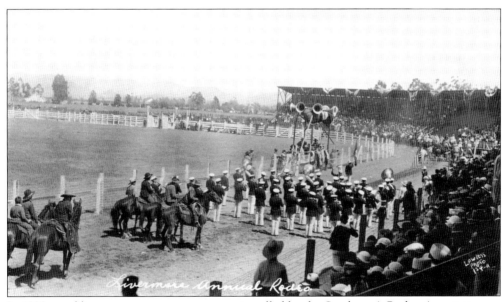

In 1930, a public announcement system was installed by the Stockmen's Rodeo Association, as shown in this photograph of the Grand Entry. Livermore's Bud Bentley was the announcer until 1965. Prior to the installation, announcing was done on horseback with a megaphone.

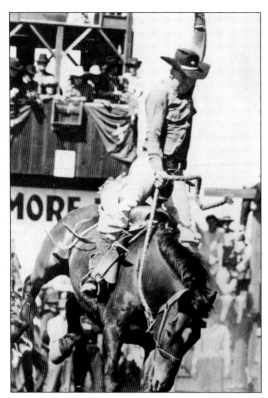

A cowboy does his best to hold onto a bucking bronco at the 1944 Livermore Rodeo in both photographs on this page. Livermore's is among the premier rodeos, with some of the toughest stock animals on the circuit. Saddle bronc riding is considered a classic event and evolved from the ranch work of breaking and training horses. It is the only event that has been on every Livermore Rodeo program since 1918.

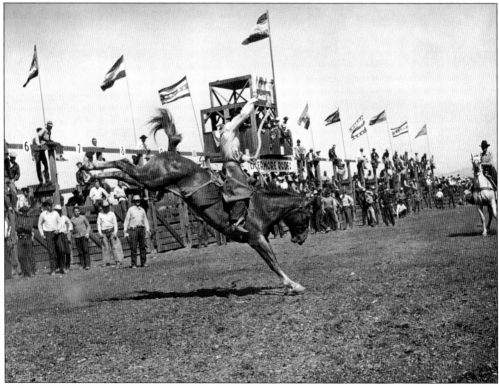

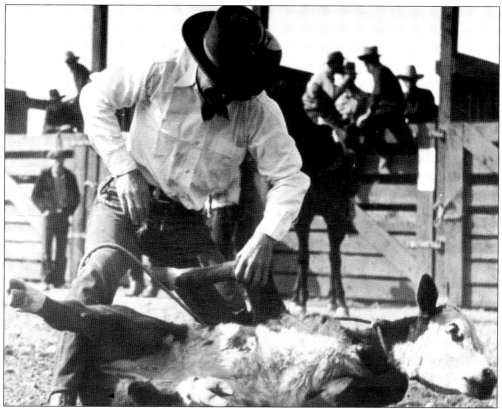

The unidentified cowboy pictured above is participating in calf roping at the 1938 Livermore Rodeo. Asbury Schell, from Tempe, Arizona, won the event that year. Calf roping was added to the program in 1931. Other popular events include bareback riding, wild cow milking, steer wrestling, team roping, barrel racing, and bull riding. Below is a c. 1930 E.J. Lawless photograph of a trick roper. The 1930 rodeo was held over the Fourth of July weekend rather than in June.

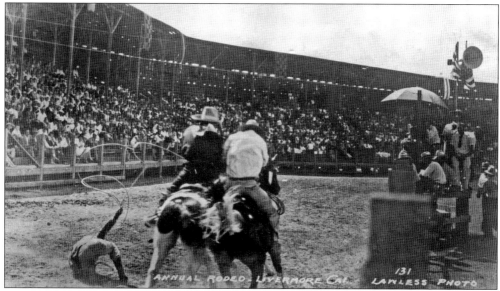

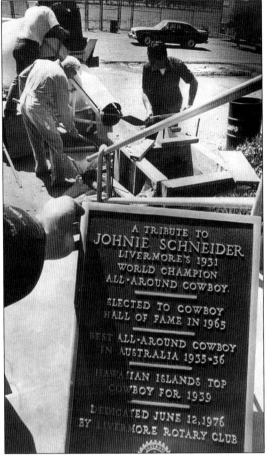

Johnie Schneider's rodeo career in Livermore began in July 1923 and continued well into the 1930s. The Johnie Schneider Kids Club was founded in 1932 and invited all youngsters to ride in the opening Rodeo Parade with 249 children partaking in the events. This plaque, dedicated to Schneider, was placed in Robertson Park in 1976 by the Rotary Club of Livermore to honor the man who embodied the cowboy spirit and the Livermore rodeo. It indicates that Schneider was elected to the National Cowboy Hall of Fame in 1965. (He was inducted into the Rodeo Hall of Fame in 1955.) A year earlier, he served as the grand marshal of Livermore's yearly Rodeo Parade to the thrill of residents and longtime fans.

The first Livermore Boy Scouts kite-flying contest winners, Celestine Tuccoli (smallest, given a prize of a flashlight), Paul Pitt (original, given a prize of a Scout axe), Jack Altamirano (highest and first prize, given a prize of a camera), and Chester Van Horn (biggest, given a prize of a Scout axe) pose in an E.J. Lawless photograph in 1930. The Boy Scouts kite-flying contests were successful well into the 1960s.

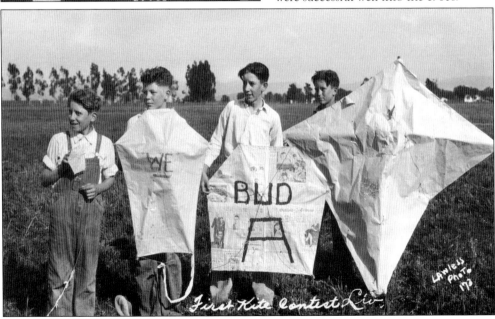

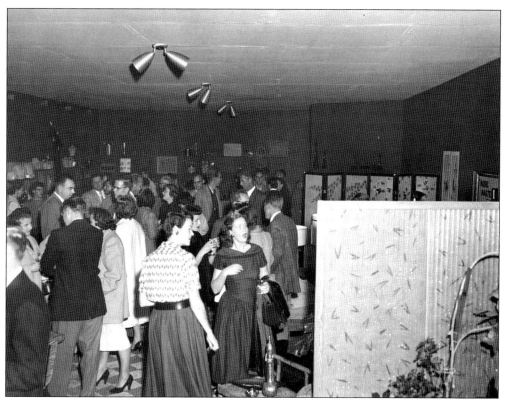

A late-1950s party is pictured at the Chequerstor, located on South L Street. In the foreground are Helen Shirley (left) and Helen Thompson.

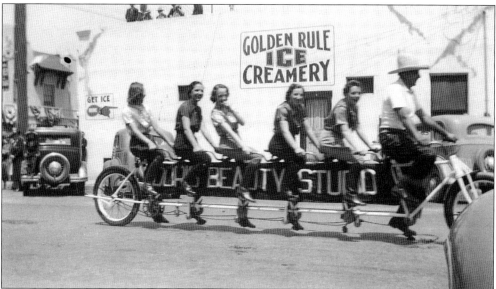

In a 1933 parade, a multi-person bicycle used for mobile advertising pedals past the Golden Rule Ice Creamery. The ice cream parlor and restaurant was a popular meeting spot for local civic organizations as well as teenagers on dates. It also would have been the place to cool off after watching the parade in the hot June sun.

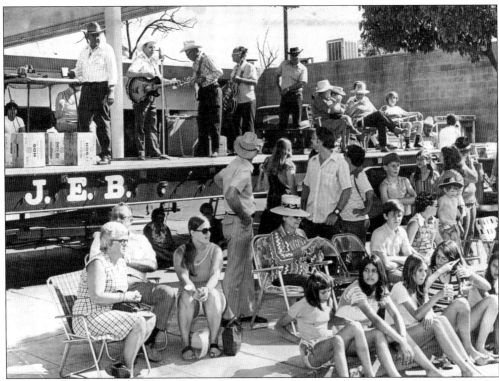

Playing to a parade crowd on a flatbed in the late 1960s, at the northeast corner of First and L Streets, these musicians provide a sound track to the festivities of the day.

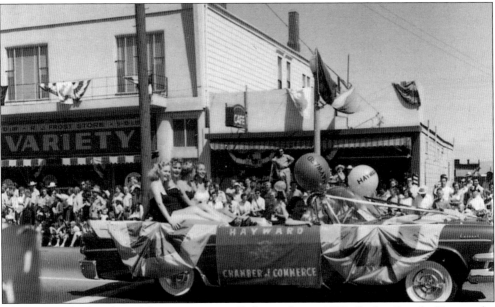

The Hayward Chamber of Commerce car rolls by in this c. 1950s Rodeo Parade. Due to the event's popularity, nearby cities sent representatives to the parade. Many prominent Hayward businessmen, like former Hayward mayor Jack Smith, played a role in the development of Livermore and surrounding communities.

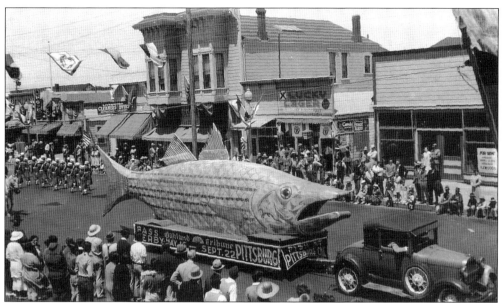

The City of Pittsburg, California, sent an entry to the 1935 Rodeo Parade. The giant fish float was an attempt to lure the people of Livermore to the North Bay to try their luck at the Bass Derby.

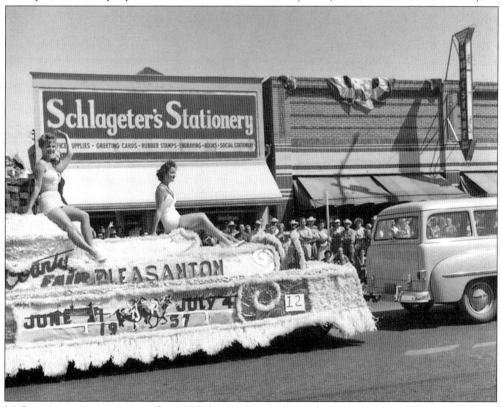

Making an appearance in the 1957 festivities are representatives from Alameda County who are taking the opportunity to advertise the Alameda County Fair at the fairgrounds in neighboring Pleasanton.

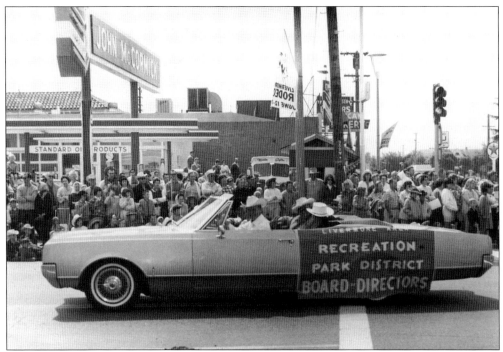

The Livermore Area Recreation and Park District (LARPD) board of directors, wearing cowboy hats, takes part in an early-1970s parade. The car is heading east on First Street near Livermore Avenue. In 1947, the LARPD, independent of the city government, was formed to focus on the mission of providing parks and programs to "stimulate, educate and enrich our lives."

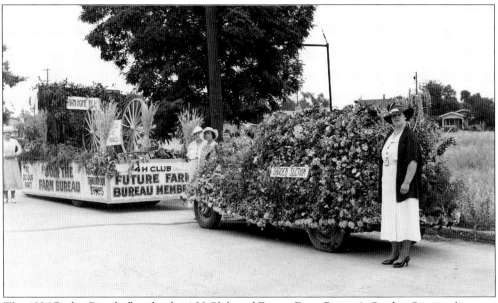

The 1936 Rodeo Parade float by the 4-H Club and Future Farm Bureau's Garden Section features, from left to right, Etta Leferoer, Ogetta Sweet, a Mrs. Ruter, and Helen Johnson. Also participating in that year's parade were California governor Frank F. Merriam and California lieutenant governor George J. Hatfield. The parade's grand marshal was Sheriff J.J. McGrath of San Mateo County.

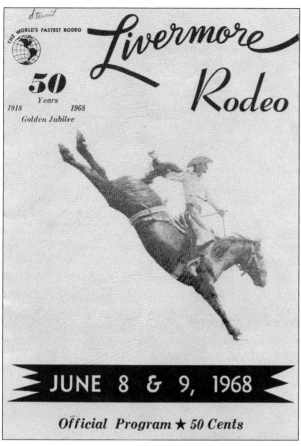

This is the 50th anniversary program for Livermore's famous "World's Fastest Rodeo" in 1968. It has only been canceled three times: in 1924, with an outbreak of hoof-and-mouth disease that wiped out hundreds of livestock; in 1959, as the wooden bleachers were deemed unsafe and condemned days before the event; and in 1961, because of a dispute between the Livermore Area Recreation and Park District and the Rodeo Association that delayed construction of the current rodeo grounds.

Photographed by Bill Elliott, 1953 Rodeo Queen Gerry Root was the daughter of Dr. and Mrs. R.R. Root. She received $100 from the rodeo association to buy her outfit and represented Livermore at other rodeos. Her father was a local veterinarian, a former director of the Livermore Rodeo Association, won trophies in stock horse competition, and also served as grand marshal of the parade that year.

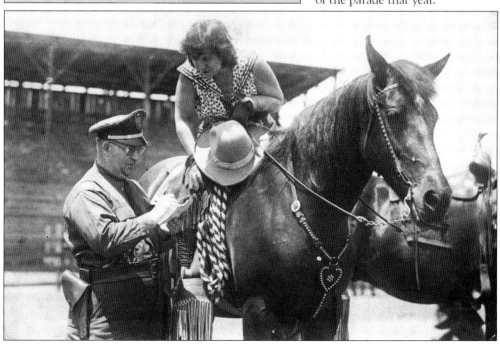

DISCOVER THOUSANDS OF LOCAL HISTORY BOOKS
FEATURING MILLIONS OF VINTAGE IMAGES

Arcadia Publishing, the leading local history publisher in the United States, is committed to making history accessible and meaningful through publishing books that celebrate and preserve the heritage of America's people and places.

Find more books like this at
www.arcadiapublishing.com

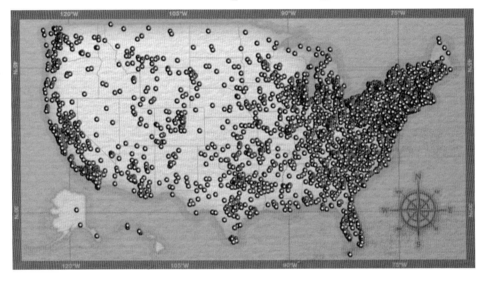

Search for your hometown history, your old stomping grounds, and even your favorite sports team.

Consistent with our mission to preserve history on a local level, this book was printed in South Carolina on American-made paper and manufactured entirely in the United States. Products carrying the accredited Forest Stewardship Council (FSC) label are printed on 100 percent FSC-certified paper.

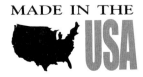

MADE IN THE USA